Outdoor Provision in the Early Years

Outdoor Provision in the Early Years

edited by
Jan White

SAGE

Los Angeles | London | New Delhi
Singapore | Washington DC

KH

First published 2011

SAGE Publications Ltd
1 Oliver's Yard
55 City Road
London EC1Y 1SP

SAGE Publications Inc.
2455 Teller Road
Thousand Oaks, California 91320

SAGE Publications India Pvt Ltd
B 1/I 1 Mohan Cooperative Industrial Area
Mathura Road
New Delhi 110 044

SAGE Publications Asia-Pacific Pte Ltd
33 Pekin Street #02-01
Far East Square
Singapore 048763

Library of Congress Control Number: 2010934531

British Library Cataloguing in Publication data

A catalogue record for this book is available from the British Library

ISBN 978-1-4129-2308-8
ISBN 978-1-4129-2309-5 (pbk)

Typeset by C&M Digitals (P) Ltd, Chennai, India
Printed by CPI Antony Rowe, Chippenham, Wiltshire
Printed on paper from sustainable resources

9/2/11

This book is dedicated to all the early years practitioners who enjoy sharing children's pleasure in being outside and who strive to create high quality experiences for as much time every day as possible.

Contents

Acknowledgements

This book has been a long time in gestation and many people have had an influence in its creation and contents.

In particular, I would like to thank the original Vision and Values group, and all those who have commented on, contributed to, endorsed and made use of the vision and values themselves.

Jane Cole and Kath Humphreys were particularly important for the comments they made very early on that sparked the whole idea of the need for shared values for outdoor play.

Peter Carne OBE and Julie Mountain, of Learning through Landscapes, drove the project to bring the early years sector together across the UK on this significant issue. A vision in itself, and thanks for giving me the responsibility for such an amazing task!

Thanks too to all the thinkers, activists and writers championing outdoor play whose work has been drawn on in compiling these values.

Jude Bowen, Senior Commissioning Editor at SAGE Publications, has shown extraordinary patience and belief in the value of this project. I'm so glad you were able to keep it alive.

I greatly appreciate my fellow authors of the book, who have also stuck in despite heavy work loads and numerous intervening events. I was warned that editing a book is not a simple thing! I'm honoured to have worked with you all.

Jane Wratten and Sue Scott so willingly provided their photographs and time, and thanks to all the settings who shared material and parents who gave permission for the use of the images of their children at play outdoors.

Liz Magraw would like to particularly thank Hind Leys Pre-school, Shepshed, Leicestershire, for the photographs and inspiration for her chapter.

Thanks must also go to Ivan Harper, senior playworker at the Yard adventure playground, and Judi Legg, playscape designer, who collaborated with Theresa Casey and the children in the sandscape design described in the case study in Chapter 9.

And of course, special thanks go to all the children who continue to inspire us and confirm how much the outdoors matters.

Foreword

There is a general understanding that young children are spending more time in early years education and care and less time playing outside when at home. This indicates that there is a need for early years settings to provide high quality experiences and well planned provision outside so that young children are able to engage with all the outdoors has to offer. Rather than being regarded as somewhere for children to let off steam, the outdoors needs to be considered as an important component of the whole setting's education and care.

During 2004 early years experts developed in partnership a shared Vision and Values for outdoor play offering Core Values for high quality outdoor experiences for young children. The values are intrinsically linked to the subjects that thread through the book and are enhanced by the authors of each chapter.

This book, with contributions by Jan White (ed.) and her team of distinguished early years experts, is a valuable asset to all professionals working with young children. Each chapter unpicks a different subject concerning young children going outside and offers links with theory as well as case studies and images that will support practitioners. It will inspire and guide them in developing their own pedagogical practice.

The specialists offer a clearly defined rationale within their own subject for why the outdoors offers young children the best possible start in life and how to offer high quality outdoor provision and experiences. Through coherent and strong content they present guidance underpinned by excellent principles that supports the need for young children to be outside in a safe and stimulating environment.

Jacky Brewer, Senior Early Years Advisor at
Learning through Landscapes

About the editor and contributors

Editor

Jan White Jan works both nationally and abroad to advocate and support high quality outdoor provision in educational services for children from birth to five, focusing on what children naturally want to do in their play and how the outdoor environment enables this. With over 25 years of experience in education, she has developed a deep commitment to the power of the outdoors to support children's well-being, learning and development.

Previously playing a key role in developing Learning through Landscapes' philosophy and support for the early years sector and associate consultant with Early Excellence, she is currently Mentor to Sandfield Natural Play Centre, where she is supporting innovative outdoor provision and practice. She is also pedagogical adviser for Play Garden, guest lecturer at Sheffield Hallam University and researches outdoor environments for early childhood at Sheffield University. Jan is author of *Playing and Learning Outdoors: Making Provision for High-Quality Experiences in the Outdoor Environment* (Routledge, 2008), and collaborated with Siren Films to produce the series of training DVDs *Babies Outdoors, Toddlers Outdoors* and *Two Year Olds Outdoors* (Siren Films, 2010).

Contributors

Theresa Casey is an independent play consultant and author with special interests in inclusion, environments for play and children's rights. In 2008 she was elected President of the International Play Association, a world-wide membership based association whose purpose is to preserve, protect and promote the child's right to play as a fundamental human right. Theresa's career has spanned adventure play for children with disabilities, developing play projects for children in disadvantaged communities with the Foundation for Child Development, Thailand, and supporting inclusion through play in schools and networks of community settings. She is known for the Play Inclusive (P.inc) Action Research project, is a fellow of the Winston Churchill Memorial Trust and her work has been recognised through a number of national and international awards. The 2nd edition of her book *Inclusive Play: Practical Strategies for Working with Children Aged 3–8* was published by SAGE in 2010 following *Environments for Outdoor Play: A Practical Guide to Making Space for Children* in 2007. She keeps her hands dirty by spending a lot of time digging up worms and rounding up snails with her two young children.

Di Chilvers has most recently worked for the National Strategies as an Adviser for the Early Years Foundation Stage. Previous to this Di was a Senior Lecturer in Early Childhood at Sheffield Hallam University where she led the BA Hons in Early

Childhood Studies and Early Years Professional courses, as well as teaching on the NPQICL. She was also involved in practitioner research projects and the MA in Early Childhood Studies. Di spent many years in Nottingham working with young children and their families in early years settings with a particular interest in play (indoors and outdoors), children's thinking and talk and child led learning. She originally trained as a Nursery Nurse, then became an early years teacher and has worked in Further Education, Higher Education and consultancy work for various authorities. She has also spent time in Ghana working with teachers in a school with 900 children where she talked about the way young children learn through play. She is the author of *Young Children Talking: The Art of Conversation and Why Children Need to Chatter* (British Association for Early Childhood Education, 2006).

Ros Garrick is a Principal Lecturer at Sheffield Hallam. She has wide professional and research experience in the field of children and young people's services, particularly in early years education and care. Ros gained professional experience as a teacher and Early Years Teacher Adviser in Leeds. She worked across the maintained and PVI sectors in both these roles. At Sheffield Hallam, Ros has taken a lead in the development of a successful Early Childhood Studies degree, a sector endorsed Early Years foundation degree and Early Years Professional Status training pathways. She has also worked as a researcher on projects focused on children's services, including early years services. Most recently she jointly directed a Department for Education project focused on young children's experiences of the Early Years Foundation Stage. Ros is author of *Playing Outdoors in the Early Years* (2nd Edition) (Continuum, 2009) and *Minibeasts and More: Young Children Investigating the Natural World* (British Association for Early Childhood Education, 2006).

Stephanie Harding was originally an archaeologist but changed career after three years living abroad in Papua New Guinea. After working in a playgroup and undertaking voluntary work at a primary school she made the decision to train as an early years teacher. She is presently a full-time teacher and the Pedagogical Team Leader at Earlham Early Years Centre in Norwich, Norfolk. She completed an MA in Early Education and Care in 2000 for which she researched a dissertation on non-verbal communication. Along with two colleagues she received a Best Practice Research Bursary to look at aspects of the dispositional curriculum developed at Earlham. When, as part of the Early Excellence programme, the centre acquired a new and enlarged outdoor learning area she used a Leadership Research Bursary to consider how the children were developing new skills and strategies to manage their learning in the new environment. As a qualified Forest School Leader she enjoys leading Forest School sessions for key groups based at the centre.

Liz Magraw is a highly experienced and passionate early years and Forest School practitioner. She presently works in Hind Leys Pre-school in Shepshed, Leicestershire, and is leading Forest School projects in schools and early years settings. She is also an independent consultant delivering training and providing support particularly in the fields of early years, outdoor learning, Forest School and personalised learning. She has now worked in education for 35 years as a teacher, an adviser and a head teacher. She has been involved in a number of research projects, including the StEPs, Statement of Entitlement to Play project, directed by Janet Moyles (Open University Press, 2001) and Silence and Presence (CARA, Creative partnerships and the DCSF, 2006). She contributed a chapter to *Again! Again! Understanding Schemas in Young Children*, edited by Sally Featherstone (A & C Black, 2008).

Miranda Murray trained as a primary school teacher and has taught in nurseries, schools and Children's Centres. She worked for Learning through Landscapes for five years as an Early Years Development Officer supporting settings and practition-ers all across the UK. This involved writing and running a variety of workshops and speaking at conferences about the importance of the outdoors for children, as well as developing and managing the West Sussex Outdoors for All project. This project involved working closely with 17 early years settings over two years to develop their outdoor provision. She is a qualified Forest School leader and writes and runs courses in Enabling Outdoor Environments at Cornwall College. She also works part time for FACE (Farming and Countryside Education), supporting schools in visiting local farms to promote learning outside the classroom. Miranda believes passionately in the right for all children to experience the special nature of the outdoors and have the opportunity to make meaningful memories there that they will recall with joy for years to come. She currently lives and works in Devon.

Felicity Thomas trained as a nursery and infant teacher at the Froebel Institute in Roehampton. Her Froebelian training has given her a passion for following and extending children's learning. She also believes in the principle of parents being their child's first educator. Felicity began her career in a nursery class in East Ham, Greater London. She has been Deputy Head and Head of Earlham Early Years Centre for the past 15 years. In this time the Centre has developed from a Nursery School, to an Early Excellence Centre and now a Children's Centre. In 2000 Felicity did a Best Practice research scholarship looking at sharing the language of disposi-tions with parents. During this research parents became instrumental in developing the disposition of playfulness. Felicity was one of the pilot cohort to study for the National Professional Qualification for Integrated Centre Leadership and as part of this went to New Zealand to study early years provision there and the application of the Te Whāriki curriculum. She continued her studies and went on to complete her Masters degree in 2007. She is an Associate Lecturer at the UEA on the Early Years Professional course and the MA in Early Years Education.

Helen Tovey is Principal Lecturer in Early Childhood Studies at Roehampton University, London. She teaches on BA, MA and CPD programmes focusing par-ticularly on aspects of play and environments for young children. She is a Froebel trained teacher and has had extensive experience of working with young children, including 10 years as a nursery school head teacher in an inner city area of London. She is the author of numerous publications on outdoor play and risk including *Playing Outdoors: Spaces and Places, Risk and Challenge* (Open University Press, 2007).

Tim Waller is Reader in Early Years Education and Coordinator of the Childhood Research Cluster at the University of Wolverhampton. Tim is also a Convener of the Outdoor Learning Special Interest Group in the European Early Childhood Education Research Association (EECERA) and an active member of the Early Years Special Interest Group in the British Educational Research Association (BERA). He was formerly Director of Postgraduate Studies in the Department of Childhood Studies at Swansea University. Previously he taught in nursery, infant and primary schools in London and has also worked in the USA. His research interests include outdoor learning, pedagogy and social justice in early childhood. Tim is Director of the Longitudinal Evaluation of the Role and Impact of Early Years Professionals (in England) – a three-year project commissioned by the Children's Workforce Development Council. Since September 2003 he has been coordinating an ongoing research project designed to investigate children's perspectives of their outdoor play. This project has involved developing and using a range of 'participatory' methods for research with young children. He has also helped to establish the Men in Childcare Network in Wales. Recently, he has edited the second edition of *An Introduction to Early Childhood: A Multi-Disciplinary Approach* (Sage, 2009).

Claire Warden is an educational consultant who has developed her approach to experiential learning through a variety of experiences. She has taken a pathway that includes working in a variety of types of centre, advisory work, and lecturing in further education. Previously a lecturer in Primary Education at Strathclyde University, in 1996 she set up Mindstretchers as an educational consultancy, which also supplies resources and publishes training materials. Claire has authored many books and materials relating to outdoors provision, including *The Potential of a Puddle, Talking and Thinking Floorbooks, Nurture through Nature, Nature Kindergartens* and *Journeys into Nature,* to enable people to work in a naturalistic way with young people. Mindstretchers run Whistlebrae Nature Kindergarten and Auchlone Nature Kindergarten for children from two to six years in Perth and Kinross, Scotland. Claire is also a European coordinator for the World Nature Collaborative, which brings together educators, landscape architects, environmentalists and health workers to support a multidisciplinary approach to outdoor educational provision. Mindstretchers is also on the consultative committee to the Scottish Government on the place of risk in learning.

Introduction

Jan White

The necessity of having vision and values for outdoor provision

Playing and interacting outdoors meets the way young children most want to be, behave, develop and learn. The kind of play we had outdoors as young children will have played a big role in influencing our attitudes and abilities as we grew up, affecting our outlook on and approach to life, as well as contributing broadly and deeply to our learning and education. Outdoor play has a potentially powerful and significant role in many fundamental aspects of young children's health and development, including all five outcomes of the Every Child Matters agenda (DCSF, 2008a).

White (2008: 2–3) asserts that play outdoors has the potential to offer children:

- access to space with opportunities to be their natural, exuberant physical and noisy selves

- fresh air and direct experience of how the elements of the weather feel

- contact with natural and living things, to maintain their inborn affinity, curiosity and fascination with all things belonging to the natural world

- freedom to be inquisitive, exploratory, adventurous, innovative and messy

- a vast range of real experiences that are relevant and meaningful and that make sense

- endless opportunities for discovery, play and talk so that new experiences can be processed, understood and used

- an environment that feeds information into all the senses at the same time

- involvement with the whole body giving deeply felt meanings and all-round physical health

- movement experiences that develop essential structures within the brain and nervous system

- emotional and mental well-being, where self image and esteem grow

- social interactions that build relationships, social skills and enjoyment of being with others

- lots of opportunities to set themselves challenges and to learn how to keep themselves safe

- a place that meets the way they learn best and allows them to express feelings, thoughts and ideas in a way more suited to them.

There is a groundswell of interest in the role of outdoor environments in early childhood education, reviving the deep roots and belief in the necessity of being and playing outdoors embedded in the English Nursery School tradition of the 19th century (Garrick, 2009). Recognition of outdoor play's place in young children's lives is not new and certainly not a current 'fad', although this is undergoing a timely and important revitalisation (see e.g. reviews by Lester and Maudsley, 2006 and Parsons, 2007). This is supported by an increased ability to visit and examine practice in other countries, especially in Scandinavia where we see provision and practice that reminds us of what we used to believe and do! However, children's lives and play worlds have changed substantially in the past 20–30 years, becoming a great deal less active, indoor-oriented and lacking in direct contact with nature, and there is now a great and urgent need for early years services to be providing our youngest children with large daily quantities of very high quality experiences outdoors.

Recently introduced and developing early years frameworks across the UK are now including expectations that young children will be offered good quality outdoor environments in order to support emotional, social, intellectual and physical development. The *Statutory Framework for the Early Years Foundation Stage* (DCSF, 2008b) in England, the *Framework for Children's Learning for 3- to 7-year-olds in Wales* (WAG, 2008), *A Curriculum for Excellence, Building the Curriculum 2: Active Learning in the Early Years* (Scottish Executive, 2007) in Scotland, *The Northern Ireland Curriculum* (CCEA, 2007) and *Aistear – the Early Childhood Curriculum Framework in Ireland* (NCCA, 2010) all include active learning and the outdoor environment as part of effective provision for the age group they cover.

However, partly due to the legacy of 'playtime' in schools and how this is seen in relation to teaching and learning, thinking about outdoor play across all parts of the sector in all of these countries is muddled and confused. Young children's access to extensive and high quality outdoor experiences is extremely variable (and commonly low), and adults are often unclear about their role outdoors or lack confidence about this aspect of early years provision. A clear framework of belief and values is required to create firm foundations for a new view and approach to outdoor play as both medium and mechanism for effective learning.

How can we develop our daily outdoor provision to make the most of this for all our children? Whenever a new approach is developing, whether different or revitalised, we must be clear about what the *vision* is, knowing just where we are aiming to go and what we are trying to achieve. Once clear about this, we can focus on gradual and sustained progress towards the vision. In order to do this, it is crucial to take time to think about, discuss, contend, argue and agree on the understandings that underpin the ideas and approaches being explored and expounded. What *values and principles* will help us to work towards our vision? What should the lived experiences of early years care and education be like for the child and the adults working with them? What do we think high quality outdoor provision is really like? What deeply held values about young children, their play outdoors, outdoor provision and our practice there do we share? And how do these values or principles influence and inform:

- what experiences we provide on a physical level (such as the features in the environment, organisational issues and the activities made available)

- what experiences we provide and the messages we send on an emotional level (such as the ethos, atmosphere, climate and culture of the setting's outdoor provision and practice)

- what experiences we provide on an intellectual level (such as what we feel and show matters to us as adults, and what we think is important regarding the education of our youngest children).

Values that underpin our ways of thinking and acting are embedded in and grow from the beliefs we hold. With respect to early childhood education, these tend to rest upon two key questions: What is our view of the young child? and, what is our view of what education at this age should really be about? However, values are not rules: rather they interact and influence each other to provide our interpretation of and position towards relevant issues and events. Our values matter: they guide our practice, giving us the starting points for making judgements about what to think and for reaching decisions about how to respond or act. Educational values need to be 'publicly explicit, justified and agreed' (Doddington and Hilton, 2007: xii). Discussions and decisions about 'what we think' collectively, as a team and as a service, are crucial in determining what we provide, how we work and how children experience being with us, and provide the basis that influences 'all those necessarily pragmatic, individual, day-to-day decisions and judgements that have to be made' (Doddington and Hilton, 2007: xiii). Ongoing discussion, review and evaluation are necessary, to ensure that the values are consciously and explicitly part of decisions both big and small, and that they serve to generate movement towards the expressed vision.

The Shared Vision & Values for Outdoor Play in the Early Years

Learning through Landscapes (LTL) has been the driving force behind the development of a strong vision about young children's access to outdoor experiences for well-being and learning and a set of clearly articulated 'core values' about what outdoor experiences should look and feel like, that is shared by the whole early years sector across England, Scotland, Northern Ireland and Wales.

Working across the UK since 1990, Learning through Landscapes campaigns on behalf of all children for better school grounds. The charity believes that:

School grounds play a vital role in every child's learning and development. They are unique spaces, providing safe and diverse opportunities for understanding, achievement, healthy exercise and play. We believe passionately that children and young people who miss out on good school grounds miss out on the best start in life. Without good school grounds, they will miss out on essential opportunities to be healthy and happy in their formative years, and to gather the experiences they need to be healthy and happy as adults. (LTL mission statement)

LTL works as a national hub for information sharing, capacity-building at local levels, advocacy and advice to government and other national organisations, and promotes innovative child-centred practice in the use, design and management of outdoor spaces in schools and settings. In line with these roles, and in response to increasing requests for support by early settings, in November 2003 LTL facilitated the bringing together of a wide range of early years specialists representing children and practitioners from Scotland, Wales and England and with high levels of expertise in quality outdoor provision and experience for young children. The intention was to enable these people and organisations to join up their perspectives and advocacy roles, to create a shared and influential voice for outdoor play in the early years. A remarkable level of common understanding and agreement about what mattered resulted in the launch and publication in 2004 of these Shared Vision statements:

- All children have the right to experience and enjoy the essential and special nature of being outdoors.

- Young children thrive and their minds and bodies develop best when they have free access to stimulating outdoor environments for learning through play and real experiences.

- Knowledgeable and enthusiastic adults are crucial to unlocking the potential of outdoors. (Vision & Values Partnership, 2004)

The shared discussions also led to strong alignment about the core values that underpin high quality outdoor play experiences for children in their early years, and, led by the editor of this book as Senior Early Years Development Officer for LTL, these were articulated together with their rationales in the same publication (Vision & Values Partnership, 2004), first published in *Nursery World* magazine (1 April 2004) and available as a copyright-free download on Learning through Landscapes' website (www.ltl.org.uk and search 'vision and values' in the resources section). The Early Years Vision and Values for Outdoor Play now forms part of the Early Years Foundation Stage guidance (DCSF, 2008b) to support the development of 'enabling environments' outdoors and can be found at http://nationalstrategies. standards.dcsf.gov.uk/node/84396 and it also has a clear role to play in supporting the Learning Outside the Classroom (LOtC) agenda (DfES, 2006). Thousands of educators, settings, parents and organisations have endorsed the Vision and Values statements via Learning through Landscapes' website, adopting them for their own use.

The shared vision and values continue to be at the centre of advocacy, training and development work to support:

- deeper understandings about the nature of powerful outdoor play

- stronger commitment to providing extensive, daily access to rich outdoor environments

- higher quality experiences for all young children, both within early childhood services and in work with parents and families.

They provide an authoritative and potent tool in both initial training and ongoing professional development for supporting all the adults who work with young children to fully understand what being, playing and learning outdoors should be about, and to provide the value base for achieving rich, satisfying and effective outdoor provision for *all* children from birth to seven.

The aims and organisation of this book

Because value-laden frameworks that are set out clearly and tested through discussion can be both strong and coherent they are able to offer not just a basis for clear and decisive action, but can also generate the will to act, by inspiring conviction in those that feel they own and hold them dear. We believe that conviction and commitment to a set of values is thus a vital part of teaching well. (Doddington and Hilton, 2007: xiii)

This book aims to:

- set out a clearly expressed set of values for outdoor provision that are both coherent and strong and that work together to achieve the vision for all young children

- offer an evidence base and informed discussion regarding each value

- encourage practitioners to think about and test the values through discussion and practice, so that the values articulate their own beliefs and principles

- illustrate how the values interlink to form a coherent framework that gives a strong sense of direction and clear 'pedagogy' for outdoor play

- stimulate enthusiasm and the desire to act on behalf of young children

- deepen understanding about the nature of play outdoors and engender commitment to achieve high quality outdoor provision

- offer strong foundations and underpinning rationales for the generation of purposeful and effective action

- support the development of rich, satisfying and memorable experiences for all young children.

Whilst principles provide a set of guidelines about an issue or concept, the word in common use also might suggest an externally applied nature. What is important about values is that they come from within, growing from the beliefs we hold. This book aims to give readers 'food and exercise' to use over time to develop and deepen their beliefs and values about young children's outdoor play. By identifying the 'big ideas' (Rich et al., 2005) of high quality outdoor experience and carefully examining them, offering educators both food for thought and 'strenuous exercise for their intellectual muscles' (Rich et al., 2008: 3) we intend for readers to internalise the values and take them as their own. This internalised ownership will enable practitioners and teams to guide their own practice, drawing on them as the shared and agreed starting points for making judgements and reaching decisions, both big and small, in their struggles and efforts to develop rich and successful outdoor play.

In this book, the emphasis is on the provision and practice of daily, on-site outdoor play. Off-site experiences are highly valuable where these form a frequent and long-term *extra layer* of outdoor provision, and especially when they take place in unstructured, natural environments (Knight, 2009: 43). What these experiences do for adults is just as significant as the benefits for children, since they tend to have a major impact upon the educator's views of young children's capabilities and upon their understandings of the nature of outdoor experience, which then alters their daily practice (Sightlines, 2008). However, it is really important that these forms of outdoor provision are not seen as *alternatives* to rich and prolonged daily experiences, making up for accepted deficits in on-site spaces, and that they provide developmental experiences for the educators that inform values, attitudes and commitment for *all* their practice (see e.g. Knight, 2009: 91–105).

Each value represents a big idea for effective practice outdoors and each is explored in its own right, chapter by chapter. Authors have brought their specialist knowledge to the issue in question, drawing widely upon thinking, research and practice in that area to open up thinking and debate regarding this element of practice for outdoor play. But clearly these ideas and values interact considerably, each informing the others. Since there are so many interactions across chapters, as editor I have not attempted to identify these links. Practitioners will benefit from reading chapters in the book more than once, so that it becomes increasingly apparent how the values work together to form a coherent whole.

The sequence in which the big ideas are presented does not signify any hierarchy of importance, and the chapters can be used in any order. Indeed moving in different ways between chapters will spark different kinds of connections in thinking, and should be very beneficial. However, the value statements as set out in the original publication (Vision & Values Partnership, 2004) do form a logical sequence for considering outdoor play provision and practice, and this sequence has been retained here.

In order to provide good food and exercise, each chapter takes a three step approach.

- The chapter first provides an 'appetiser' by considering **why** this issue matters to and for young children, making the case for this value being a *fundamental component* of effective and successful outdoor experience for children from birth to five and beyond. It is here that much of the research evidence is presented.

- The writer then goes on to offer the main course by exploring **what** this value means for policy, provision and practice and what it might look like in real life, drawing out where appropriate issues and examples relevant to different age groups. Chapters take different forms in this section depending upon the nature of the value being examined. Here you will find prompts for thinking, issues and questions, advice and ideas, examples of practice and case studies.

- The final section takes on the role of provoking 'exercise' for intellectual and physical muscles, through suggesting things to read, things to think about and discuss and things to do, so that the big idea contained in the chapter can be debated, argued, tested and owned. This section also aims to offer starting points for **how** settings can move towards achieving this aspect of practice, from easily achieved, small and immediate steps to take, to longer-term developments.

Each of the authors has played a significant role as a champion for learning and developing through outdoor play in early childhood, has written extensively on outdoor provision, and brings specific experience, knowledge and understanding to the theme of their chapter.

The underpinning value

Underpinning all the chapters in this book is the deeply held belief that the outdoors has huge value for young children and that the outdoor environment in early years settings is just as important as the indoors. It therefore must have equal status in all provision for young children.

> Value: Young children should be outdoors as much as indoors and need a well-designed, well-organised, integrated indoor-outdoor environment, preferably with indoors and outdoors available simultaneously (Vision & Values Partnership, 2004).

Outdoors is essential and must be given equal status, equal time and equal thinking to the indoors

Outdoor provision is an essential part of the child's daily environment and life, not an option or an extra. Being, playing and interacting outdoors has just as much value for children as doing these things indoors; in fact, it could be argued that it actually has more value, especially for young children and particularly for some individuals. The outdoors is a powerful learning environment which the young child is strongly attuned to and which provides multi-sensory, movement-based, holistic and stimulating experience that matches the way they learn best. It also has a significant role to play in mental and physical health. Therefore, outdoor space must be considered a necessary part of an early years environment, and young children must have substantial access to an outdoor environment *every* day, throughout the year.

> Frequent lack of attention to the external environment must come from some bizarre assumption that knowledge acquired indoors is superior to that gained outside. (Bruce, 1987: 55)

If being outdoors is so beneficial, the outdoor environment must be viewed as having equal status with the indoors as a place for learning and development, providing a different set of experiences, meeting different needs and the same needs in a different way. If outdoor play is to be rich, satisfying and productive, and have this equal status, it must receive equal attention and effort in commitment, time, organisation, planning, assessment, and so on. However, because many outdoor environments are not as well developed as their indoor counterpart in the same setting, it may well be that the outdoor environment currently requires *more* thought, attention, time and effort. The outdoor space must be well thought through and well organised to maximise its value and usability by children and adults, making best use of its special nature. 'For outdoor play to be successful it is crucial that the outdoor environment is considered in as much depth as any other educational setting' (Bilton, 2002: 2).

Observation, documentation, interpretation and decisions about adult responses are just as important and as vital a part of practice as they are indoors, and this should be one of the main roles of educators outside. When adults do this outdoors, they come to realise just how powerful children's thinking and learning is in the contexts that the outdoors provides, resulting in an upward spiral in understanding, attitude and enthusiasm.

Giving outdoor play equal status to indoor play means that attention is given to ensuring that it is a rich, stimulating environment that provides access to all aspects of whatever curriculum the setting aspires to offer. When practitioners are confident that this is the case, they feel more comfortable in offering children long periods of time in this environment. This sets up a positive feedback cycle, in which children's play develops in depth and quality and it becomes a more positive and productive place for learning (also improving play indoors), and therefore raising its status with educators, parents and children. With more time and a richer environment, children's behaviour is calmer, less frenetic and boisterous, quieter children are less overwhelmed and popular resources cause less anxiety and conflict; there is less fragmentation to the day allowing children to settle into sustained and rewarding play; higher levels of concentration and persistence with more sustained and deeper thinking can develop, and more opportunity to wallow in *free-flow play* exists. Children do not get involved in long-term, deeper quality construction and role play when they know they will have to stop and clear away: 'to concentrate and persevere, children need to know that the time is available to do so' (Bilton, 2002: 12).

Prolonged daily access accelerates confidence-building and skill acquisition, since children do not spend so much time settling from the move from indoors. This reduces the possibility of accidents, deepens the use of resources and gives children much more opportunity to build on previous experiences, generating bigger ideas and projects.

Outdoors forms half of a combined indoor–outdoor environment in the early years

The whole curriculum can and should be available outside: it is a complete learning environment. However, how this curriculum is offered and accessed outdoors must be very different to how it is provided indoors – attempting to repeat what is done successfully indoors will not be effective and is a misguided and seriously missed opportunity. The richness of the outdoor environment, although substantial in itself, is even greater when the inside and outside are considered as a combined environment. Each half of the indoor–outdoor environment offers significantly different, but complementary, spaces, experiences and ways of being to young children. Harnessing the strengths of each place brings so much more to the play and learning opportunities the setting can provide.

Viewing the two spaces – each with different atmospheres and different opportunities – as two equal-status and complementary halves of a combined environment results in staff putting more thought and effort into the outdoor provision, leading to higher quality experiences and interactions. When the outdoors is used for what it is able to offer best, this may result in less need indoors to offer everything, so that, in turn, it can be better used for what *it* does well. Limited space indoors, which is not uncommon, is much ameliorated by being able to use each half of the combined environment to its strengths. For example, sand and water play work so much more effectively outdoors that it may not be necessary to provide these indoors, as is the case in most Scandinavian preschools.

The vision must be for a simultaneously available combined indoor–outdoor environment

> The adults planning for the class should be thinking about the indoor and outdoor areas not as separate spaces but as linked areas where a child involved in an activity may move between them, using the equipment and resources which best meet her or his needs where and when the play requires them. (Lasenby, 1990, quoted in Bilton, 2002: 9)

Outdoor and indoor spaces should be available simultaneously and be experienced in a joined-up way, with each being given equal status and joint attention for their contribution to young children's well-being, health, stimulation and all areas of development. When children can move between the two halves of their play environment, making the most of what each place can provide, a calmer, richer, more stimulating, more responsive and more productive learning environment is created. Lower numbers of children are inside and outside at any one time, reducing issues with overcrowding and sharing; more space and a greater range of opportunities are available at any one time; children will not be changing clothes all at the same time in a small space; and sudden weather changes are less problematic and can be exploited more easily. Simultaneous access provides the generosity of time that young children need so much.

Practitioners should think beyond how the two environments differ so as to harness their strengths, to how the two spaces can work to support each other, and plan for experiences that join the two environments up. For example, increased richness in play and learning come from a simple planned linkage between writing letters and wrapping parcels indoors to collecting, sorting and delivering them outdoors (especially if they are presents delivered by Santa!).

Here are some things that need to be well thought through in order for the outdoors to operate as a full-status half of the environment.

- *Beliefs and attitudes:* Positive attitudes born of deep belief are the key to positive thinking to overcome limitations and barriers.

- *Policy and procedures:* These articulate the setting's beliefs and approaches.

- *Organisation of time*: During which parts of the day is the outdoor environment available? Starting and finishing the day outside can support more comfortable transitions from home for many children, and parents get to see outdoor learning in action for their child. Does the snack have to be at a set time; does it have to be indoors?

- *Transition between inside and outside*: How can you maximise the ease of movements between the two halves? How can you create linkage so that play flows across the two spaces? Can children move resources between in and out?

- *Weather:* Organisation to ensure that it is a resource and not a hindrance is crucial, as is easy, independent access to clothing for all eventualities throughout the year.

- *Organisation:* How is the outdoor environment structured to facilitate child-led play and learning across the curriculum? A continuous provision approach with excellent storage, organisation and mobility of resources and flexibility is key here.

- *Planning and resourcing:* Plan across the two environments together, making the most of the strengths of each half of the combined environment and seeking ways for them to work in harmonious, complementary ways.

- *Flexible deployment of staff:* All staff being enthusiastic about being outdoors with children, and being prepared to change roles or move flexibly between inside and outside, depending on where children are and what they are doing.

- *Management:* What do the practitioners need to be doing day-by-day and moment-by-moment to ensure the effective operation of the environment and the fulfilment of intentions? As Bilton (2010) advises, organisation and management are closely linked and must be considered equally inside and outside. There is a vast amount to be gained from children helping to set up and clear away – it does not have to be done all at once.

The values presented for consideration in this book must become embedded in thinking so as to inform practice at all levels:

- They must be fully represented in the service's outdoor provision *policy*, and visible in the position statement, rationale and procedures relating to outdoor provision and practice.

- They must form the basis of thinking about *design*, maintenance and any developments of the outdoor spaces, and how they link to indoor spaces.

- They are vital in informing the huge range of decisions about the *organisation* of the outdoor environment itself (provision, layout, storage, when and how it is used as part of the overall provision).

- They are critical in all decisions about what *experiences* the outdoor provision is intended to offer the children using it and in planning further experiences based on observation.

- They must be drawn on to make judgements and decisions regarding the day-to-day *management* of provision and children's experience.

- They will drive interpretations and responses in minute-by-minute *interactions*.

- They should be referred to in order to review and *evaluate* each of these layers of practice.

Developing a strong framework of shared beliefs and values is fundamental to achieving the vision of meeting every child's entitlement and requirement for rich, meaningful, satisfying, effective and productive outdoor play. Adults working with young children will find that this process makes the job a great deal more meaningful, enjoyable and rewarding too!

Further reading and resources

Doddington, C. and Hilton, M. (2007) *Child-Centred Education: Reviving the Creative Tradition.* London: Sage.

Bilton, H. (2010) *Outdoor Learning in the Early Years: Management and Innovation* (3rd edn). Abingdon, Oxon & New York: Routledge.

1

The role of play

Play outdoors as the medium and mechanism for well-being, learning and development

Felicity Thomas and Stephanie Harding

This chapter explores:

- **Finding stimulation, well-being and happiness through play**
- **The development of children intellectually, physically and emotionally**
- **How children learn outdoors: physically, cognitively, emotionally, socially and spiritually**

Value: Play is the most important activity for young children outside.

Outdoor play matters to children because it offers alternative opportunities for physical, emotional, cognitive and spiritual growth compared to the built environment. Play is the means through which children find stimulation, well-being and happiness, and through which they grow physically, intellectually and emotionally. Play is the most important thing for children to do outside and the most relevant way of offering learning outdoors. The outdoor environment is very well suited to meeting children's needs for all types of play, building upon first-hand experiences.

What does 'play' mean today? It is a word that is used all the time and because of this has little meaning. The Collins dictionary has 38 different definitions. There is much to read about play theory, but not a lot of definition. Perhaps this is because play is individual and elusive and therefore cannot be generalised in a definition. Helenko, as quoted by Holme and Massie (1970), saw as an essential difficulty of defining play that it could not be isolated from other more definable activities.

However, whatever we mean by play there is a long tradition of valuing the educational importance of play, nature and the outdoors, and this became most explicit when

Friedrich Froebel's students started to settle in England and establish kindergartens from the middle of the 19th century (Garrick, 2009; Lawrence, 1969). At this time, the *garden* was seen as a place to nurture children's spiritual as well as their cognitive and physical understandings and skills. Margaret McMillan (1919) continued this tradition in her work with young children, but her emphasis was on building up their emotional and physical health and resilience. Susan Isaacs' (1930) work at the Malting House School in Cambridge continued to value the particular importance of the outdoors as a context for cognitive and affective development. In the later part of the 20th century this emphasis was lost for a while but is now reasserting itself in England through the mechanism of the Early Years Foundation Stage (EYFS) curriculum (DCSF, 2008b). The Forest School movement, which strives to support children's confidence and self-esteem as well as co-operative skills (Knight, 2009; Murray and O'Brien, 2005), and government-funded initiatives, such as the Play Builder programme, that are addressing the need for unstructured play and physical exercise (Brady et al., 2008), both recognise the role of outdoor play in supporting children's learning and development.

Tina Bruce has very much informed the view of play developed at our centre and her definition of *free-flow play* below explains how play is utilised as a mechanism for learning:

> We can say that free-flow play seems to be concerned with the ability and opportunity to wallow in ideas, experiences, feelings and relationships. It is also about the way children come to use the competencies they have developed. It is the way children integrate all their learning... (Bruce, 1991: 42)

This idea of play being a mechanism for the integration of learning is especially relevant to what takes place outdoors, and the reason for this is the greater autonomy children have both to direct their learning and to interpret their sensory experiences. The natural world is more controlled by the weather, season and temperature than by the human hand, and this means that the learning potential is both broader and deeper because it has not been limited by one or more person's ideas or ethos relating to the process of education.

'Playfulness' is one of the most important dispositions to support children's learning and we feel children have to be able to be doing the following to be 'playful':

- understanding imaginary worlds

- being a playful partner with both children and adults

- exploring opportunities for imaginary or pretend play with a range of materials and found objects

- observing positive and mutually respectful relationships

- actively taking risks in playing and developing self management

- developing the ability to make choices

- playing spontaneously initiated games

- moving towards a sensitive awareness of verbal and non-verbal play signals

- embracing creative thinking.

Every day children play in the garden doing these things. The outdoors provides an environment which allows children to freely explore their feelings, ideas and relationships, supporting their learning and development through using the natural world to stimulate and shape their play.

So what does learning and developing through play look like in the outdoors?

In considering play and its role in learning it can be useful to focus on different areas of development, while still acknowledging the holistic nature of play and that any episode of play would be embracing more than one, and possibly all of these areas at the same time.

Physical learning

Physical learning in the outdoors has been given heightened importance recently with current concerns around child obesity, but physical exercise and movement is closely linked to cognitive development. Physical activity increases the flow of blood to the brain and thereby benefits brain activity, and the use of tools and large equipment or resources encourages the development of fine motor skills and hand/ eye coordination. Just as importantly, children learn about the world around them through movement – what Piaget called 'thought in action'. Children need to experience the world through their senses and movement before they can develop 'mental maps' and abstract thought. The outdoors as a place to learn offers more, and a greater range of, sensory and movement opportunities. In particular, it allows for larger scale movements and more spontaneous, faster, louder expression of these. In addition it offers whole-body experience of cause and effect, such as the influence of gradient on movement when sliding down a slide in different ways. These opportunities for access to fresh air and whole-body movement also encourage increasing robustness, spatial understanding, muscular control and *proprioception* (body awareness). In play outdoors there are opportunities for using large whole-body movements in imaginative and symbolic play, and particularly in superhero play. It also provides a context for rough and tumble play which is closely linked to self-management, self-control and collaborative play. In the outdoors children can set their own challenges, which are often complex and requiring problem solving and creative thinking rather than a fixed outcome. This supports what Craft (2002) describes as 'little c creativity' and 'life-wide resourcefulness' which strongly underpin more formal approaches to learning.

Cognitive learning

Problem solving around real activities promotes cognitive learning. The garden encourages greater observation and attention, and stimulates curiosity by its provision of a great diversity of sensory information that changes on a daily and sometimes

Image 1.1   Stamping in a puddle

hourly basis. For example, a child visiting the same site six times may see it differently each time because of changes in season, vegetation, weather and temperature. This can prompt a range of observations, investigations, questions and hypotheses. An increased understanding of the natural world springs from closer experience and is associated with observation skills. Outdoor provision which is diverse and varied includes support for this area of knowledge at a sensory level as well as at a knowledge and skills level. Children are able to feel the wind on their face, hear the grass whispering, see leaves changing colour, appreciate the fragility of flowers. They can smell rain, flowers and herbs. They can gain an understanding of the food chain by planting seeds, watching them grow, harvesting them and savouring and comparing the tastes, and they can observe, handle and care for living creatures. With this quantity and great diversity of sensory information they are more likely to be able to make connections with other sensory experiences and learning in other contexts.

 Case study – Jake went up the hill

Jake, aged 3 years, constantly played with the water at the top of the hill. He spent a long time pouring water down the pipe and running down the hill to see it arrive in the beach area. However, the water always got there first. Jake wanted the water to constantly go down the pipe so he could watch it arrive in the beach. The adult asked him questions to provoke his thinking.

(Continued)

(Continued)

A: Why doesn't the water go down the pipe?

J: Because it goes down there (pointing down the hill.)

A: Why does it go down there?

J: Because it does.

A: How could you stop it going down there?

J: Make a wall.

A: What could you make a wall with?

This started Jake experimenting with things in the garden which might make a wall. Firstly he collected dandelions and daisies in a wheel barrow and tipped them in place. They were washed away. The adult asked more provoking questions. He next tried twigs, leaves and grasses. These also were washed away. He then brought bark chippings and these too were washed away. Over a number of weeks he looked for heavier and heavier things to make into a wall until he decided to try the large logs that were scattered around the garden. These were heavy and took a lot of effort to move. He got his friend Cassie to help him. When the logs were in place, he found that the water washed around them and under them. Again the adult asked more questions and encouraged him to observe what was happening. Eventually he started to transport the sand from the beach area up to the stream, again with Cassie's help. Together they made walls with wet sticky sand which kept the water from flowing down the hill, but as the dammed water got higher and stronger the sand started to crumble and parts of the dam would flow away. Again the adult asked questions around,

A: I wonder how could you stop the sand falling down?

A: I wonder what would keep the sand together?

These were difficult questions. The adult produced some different materials such as plastic, leather, felt and paper. Jake wrapped the materials around the walls of sand. The adult made some bags of different sizes and left them in the beach area. Jake saw them at once and told his friend Cassie to fill them up with sand. He then carried the bags of sand up to the stream and positioned them across the stream to make a dam. The bags and sand held. He had found a way to make the water go constantly down the pipe.

Jake continued for the rest of the year to work with the sand bags and stream. He had understood that by positioning the bags in different places he could make the water in the stream flow down many various paths. Through real experience he had learnt about water flow and how 'man' can divert and change this flow. Jake had been supported by an adult who was sensitive to his play, who had informed her understanding through close observation and who guided, but never directed or inhibited, his thinking.

Jake demonstrated many of Froebel's principles as defined by Bruce (2009):

- *Practice should begin where the learner is*. It was Jake's interest that started and sustained this learning.

- *We must link, and interconnectedness is crucial.* Jake was learning about all the properties of the objects he found to build his dam and how some of them worked better together.

- *Children need both freedom and guidance, according to the laws of opposition.* Jake was free to follow his own ideas but was supported in this through guidance, not instruction, from the adult.

- *Children should, at every stage, be that stage.* The expectation of the adult was completely led by Jake's growing understanding.

- *We should live with our children.* The adult had closely observed Jake throughout the year to enable her to support and guide his thinking and learning.

- *Play holds the source of all that is good.* This activity consumed Jake's play for a whole year and led to deep level learning.

- *The only competition is with yourself.* It was Jake's desire to know and understand more that led to him fulfilling this task. It had nothing to do with anyone else's requirement of him.

Jake learnt through his play about making choices; he took risks and organised a friend to help him. He made real discoveries through experimenting and observing.

The larger the area and more varied the topography, the more opportunities are provided to develop and consolidate increasingly complex mental mapping of the area and spatial awareness (Palmer and Birch, 2004). For example:

> *Harvey takes a group of children into the woods, 'follow me' he says.*
>
> *He turns to the adult and says, 'we are finding the dragon'.*
>
> *Harvey is being a leader. He is using his imagination and creating a dragon story which other children can take part in. He is confident and assured. He is able to communicate his own thoughts and ideas. He understands that 'the woods' may hold danger and is clear about leading the other children into this area. This was a spontaneously initiated game.*

Complementing this are the opportunities to support individual children's learning styles and schemas (Athey, 1990), especially transporting (using bags, buggies and wheelbarrows), connecting (using ropes), trajectory (using wheeled vehicles and tools such as hammers and spades) and enclosure (den-making and role play). It also provides a context for making many collections of items and thereby supporting the beginning of the concepts of classification and ordering.

Role play in the garden has a different quality in that it can involve more travelling and more physical movement and expression. It also stimulates more imaginative transformations. For example, Ellie found some straight twigs and then looked carefully to find some circular seed heads. She attached the seed heads to the twigs and presented them to a friend as a gift of a lollipop. Other children used sticks as wands and as their superhero weapons. There is also more flexibility in the play in terms of being able to move and flow easily from investigative to imaginative play and back. For example, on a dewy autumn day children carefully observed the spiders' webs in the bushes and trees and then these became the evidence of

Image 1.2   Pattern making with natural materials

'baddies'; but when they saw the spiders move on the webs, they returned to observation and hypothesis regarding the spider's role. Associated with role play is the different quality and use of language in the garden. Large distances and the opportunity to use loud sounds without offending others gives language use other dimensions. Often children who use little language indoors are encouraged to be more verbal by the space and quality of the outdoors, while those who are articulate use a richer range of language and are stimulated to engage in conversation inspired by their sensory experiences (Murray and O'Brien, 2005). Children can transfer their play from the indoors to the outdoors in a way that deepens and enriches their learning.

 Case study – Bill's xylophone

Bill enjoyed playing the xylophone in the classroom, spending time watching adults and children play. He went into the garden and collected lots of logs of a similar cylindrical shape and size. He carefully arranged the logs around the inner ring of a large tractor tyre. He found himself a stick and sat in the middle of the logs to play his xylophone.

Bill was making his own imaginary world and exploring opportunities for pretend play with a range of found objects. He was transferring his knowledge from one experience to another. He was developing the ability to make choices. He carefully selected the sizes of logs he needed. He was embracing creative thinking.

Image 1.3   Exploring the properties of snow

Linked to the sensory nature of the garden is a more scientific aspect of learning; the opportunity to observe changes in materials, such as ice melting, compost decaying, seeds sprouting and clay hardening. Often these have an element of time or sequence related to seasonal change or life cycles, and this too is an important aspect of learning and acquiring knowledge.

Emotional learning

Emotional learning is supported in the garden through a direct link with sensory experience, as Tovey (2007: 16) explains: 'We learn about a place by touching, feeling, seeing, smelling, hearing it and responding emotionally. The connection between our sense and our emotions can remain powerfully evocative throughout our lives.'

In the outdoors children can also re-live experiences through their most natural channel, which is movement. This is supported by the autonomy that is more readily provided outdoors, and this in turn promotes trust and therefore rising self-esteem and confidence in their abilities. Children are more likely to be encouraged and supported to take risks and to self-manage their behaviour, enabling them to challenge themselves, to set and test their own boundaries, to understand more clearly about assessing risk, and to build resilience. Relationships with other children and with other living things are different in the outdoors. There is a necessity to appreciate other living things and their needs in a natural environment, but also opportunities for more physical testing of relationships with each other, as in rough and tumble play. The older children support and encourage the younger children by being aware of their needs, for example:

On the large climbing apparatus a child says, 'the little ones can't reach the bars, I'm going to get some blocks for them to stand on'.

This child is showing understanding and empathy with the younger children; she wants to help and encourage them. She knows how to do this as her learning in this area has been very recent. She is motivated to help and support them. She has a positive and mutually respectful relationship with them. She is supporting them to actively take risks.

Importantly, because of its size and the variety of spaces it can provide, the garden should offer opportunities for solitude and reflection (Storr, 1989). For some children, the furniture, noise, enclosed space and busyness of the classroom limits their access to quiet space in which they can be reflective or actively engaged in imagining and exploring. The garden should be able to provide for solitude and tranquillity in terms of its flexible space and its openness to the sky.

Social learning

Social learning is supported in the garden by the need to co-operate and work together, often on the real and meaningful tasks associated with maintaining the environment, such as moving sand or manure and cultivating and watering plants. These real tasks give opportunities for authentic questions, collaboration and the co-construction of ideas between children and adults, and help promote a community of learners. The best provision for outdoor play allows children more freedom

Image 1.4   Making soup together

to experiment, trusting them to do things for themselves. Because the adults are not able to control the environment in every way there is potential for a more relaxed approach to observing, rather than controlling, children's play. Children are often teachers both to their peers and to adults in terms of knowledge, but also in their uninhibited awe in response to the natural world.

Spiritual learning

In the garden there are also opportunities for spiritual learning and this provides a direct link with Froebel's thoughts about the unity of all things. Children can experience being part of an organic whole, understanding the importance of sustainability as well as developing a relationship with the natural world; they are able to feel and understand the interconnectedness of living things and appreciate their place in the world (Carson, 1998). Outdoor environments offer opportunities for engaging with and appreciating the natural world and its diversity in a way that indoors cannot. This sort of experience helps children respect life in a general sense, giving a perspective and sense of scale about how people fit into this world. Opportunities for experiencing awe and wonder at life abound in the natural environment and outdoors can also provide, if carefully planned, places to experience tranquillity and space for reflection, which are important for those children whose lives are especially noisy and chaotic.

Moving forwards

 Things to think about and do

- Share memories of the things you most liked to do outside in your childhood play and your favourite places for play. What were these places like; what materials were best for this play; who else was involved in your play? How do these memories make you feel now?

- Consider how this kind of play has contributed to the person you are now and the attributes, skills and dispositions you now have. Does the way you view and deal with life now have roots in the learning and development that took place through your childhood play outdoors?

- Review the examples of play outdoors given in this chapter and discuss just how much significant learning was taking place, especially regarding the development of positive, playful dispositions.

- Review how much unstructured and uninterrupted time the children in your setting have for their own play in the outdoor environment and whether this should and could be extended.

- Observe and document what takes place in some sustained play episodes (video is very useful). Analyse these collaboratively with other practitioners and parents to gain perspectives and understanding as to what is really

(Continued)

(Continued)

significant for the child and what deep level learning is occurring. What elements of the environment and adult support stimulated and sustained the play – could these be harnessed further to support children's play?

- Use the list from page 13–14 to help you make the outdoor play experiences of the children in your setting more 'playful' and to develop playfulness as a learning disposition.

Key messages

- Play is the most important thing for young children to do outside.

- Outdoor play matters to children because it offers alternative opportunities to the indoors that best match their ways of playing.

- Play is the means through which children find stimulation, well-being and happiness.

- Play is the most relevant way of offering learning outdoors, and is the medium and mechanism through which children grow physically, intellectually and emotionally.

- Play is the way children make connections in their learning and understanding.

- The outdoor environment is very well suited to meeting children's needs for all types of play, building upon first-hand experiences.

Further reading and resources

Bruce, T. (1991) *Time to Play in Early Childhood*. London: Hodder Stoughton.

Harding, S. (2005) 'Outdoor Play and the Pedagogic Garden', in *The Excellence of Play* (2nd edn), edited by Janet Moyles. Maidenhead: Open University Press.

Ouvry, M. (2003) *Exercising Muscles and Minds: Outdoor Play and the Early Years Curriculum*. London: National Children's Bureau.

2

Following children's interests

Child-led experiences that are meaningful and worthwhile

Liz Magraw

This chapter explores:

- **Identifying children's interests**
- **Planning provision for the short and long term**
- **The benefits of provision that is specific to children**

Value: Outdoor provision can, and must, offer young children experiences which have a lot of meaning to them and are led by the child

The strategies to identify children's interests are well known: listening to parents/carers' view of their child; talking with the child, and observing the child. These are simple but require humanity and understanding. Observation is the most powerful tool in the hands of an experienced practitioner. A misconception can arise amongst practitioners that observations impede actual involvement with children. However, observations are a requisite of good practice, informing planning, adult involvement and a relevant environment.

Quality observations go beyond the descriptive aspect of seeing, using existing knowledge of the child, as well as understanding of learning and of child development. Observations are no use to anyone, child or adults, unless acted upon. Valuable observations, once analysed, give clear lines of action:

- further observations to clarify findings

- communication with child, parents and/or other practitioners

- facilitating the interest via provision and/or role-modelling

- reflection.

To make relevant interpretations, practitioners have tools and knowledge available, such as schemas (Featherstone et al., 2008), multiple intelligences (Gardner, 1999), learning styles, emotional literacy, well-being and involvement. An inclusive approach also considers gender, cultural/ethnic diversity, special needs and gifted and talented (Sutherland, 2008).

Engagement with children incorporates continual observations; their quality and relevance are far superior when adults are fully involved in children's play. Skilful practitioners work on different levels simultaneously using strategies of involvement, observation, challenge and stepping back.

Observations should trigger a number of adult reactions, immediate or subsequent; often both.

 Case study – Adult reaction

Some children playing with water transported water in containers. Two children (4 yrs) argued over the last container available. The practitioner's immediate reaction was to help them fetch more containers, resolving the pressing issue and giving them choices.

Next she set up guttering, pipes, more tubs, adding a further dimension to transporting. Children with a trajectory schema also became interested in water moving down pipes.[1]

Children watched her putting pebbles in channels: they then began experimenting with different objects, continuing all week.

Observing two children, and the subsequent provision for them, yielded possibilities for others, extending their play and interests. With the child at the centre, the curriculum is not prescriptive, but rather a pedagogical tool.

To plan provision based on children's interests, outdoors must be given equal status to indoors, matched in quality and equally valued by adults. Children should experience life first-hand, not have it lived for them. This requires adults at ease with the outdoor environment to:

• role-model positively

• comprehend children's absorption in nature

• respect and empower children there

• stimulate their interests.

Only then can children learn to be in control, making their own decisions and facing new experiences with equanimity.

Provision and extensions might happen over short periods, so continual observation is crucial, otherwise key stages of children's development could be missed.

Case study – Provision for Sanjeev

Children with a connection schema love string. Sanjeev (5 yrs) spent a day absorbed practising knotting. Other children went over/under ropes he attached. String was made prevalent the next day. Sanjeev went straight outside, tying ropes over a larger area and, having noticed other children's interest, encouraged them to pass under. All week, string influenced play: making webs, cutting, tying, playing horses and being alpinists climbing from a ditch, unrolling string balls...

Outdoors provided vital space. Children learned to tie knots: adults intervened positively, supporting their learning and encouraging proficient children to demonstrate and impart skills, their expertise recognised and valued by adults and children.

The breadth of expertise that can be nurtured outdoors is unlimited, promoting the 'expert' children's self-esteem, peers' respect, and status within the setting's community. Outdoors, children with a naturalist intelligence (Gardner, 1999) especially have a context to showcase their skills and knowledge.

Provision and extension might happen over long periods, underpinned by ongoing observation and reflection.

 Case study – Elena's self-esteem

Elena (4½ yrs) has low self-esteem. An agile tree climber, she can work a safe route up and down, going very high. One day, she supported her twin brother climbing a tree, directing him verbally, always ahead, preserving her supremacy. Concentrating on him, she was unaware how high she had reached. She guided him down, but then became unsure. A practitioner climbed to her, talking reassuringly and pointing a descent route. This unlocked her fear; she descended independently, leaving the practitioner 'stranded'. Once down, they both laughed. Elena recalled this daily: 'Remember when you got me down?'

She gained a sense of pride and self-esteem. Her well-being rose rapidly (Laevers et al., 2006). We were able to support her developing strategies to cope with her mood swings. Acceptance and encouragement of her climbing skills led to a close relationship with another excellent climber, Georgina. Returning from the woods, she asked to hold someone's hand, wishing to belong to the group. A practitioner heard the rejection and suggested, 'Ask Georgina, a brilliant climber like you!' She did, and ever since they have spent much time together.

To support these girls and the increasing numbers interested in climbing, the setting created a climbing frame with felled trees. All children with an interest in climbing, construction and knotting were involved, as were parents. A resource inspired and instigated by a few children's interest yet benefiting all, it is a now a hive of activity, becoming a prominent feature and serving all abilities from

Image 2.1   The climbing frame

walking a floor-log to scaling heights. The timely intervention brought two girls together, united in their interest.

Communicating approval, verbally or non-verbally, supports children pursuing their interests, giving them 'permission'.

> *Some children (2 yrs) love burying things deep in sand. Never frowning upon it, adults join in. Consequently, practitioners organised treasure hunts, leading some children to express interests in treasure maps and pirates.*

> *Dug by 3- to 5-year-old children, practitioners and parents, the sandpit met the needs of 'diggers'. The children wanted a 'beach', so elements such as driftwood were added for a seaside feel.*

A setting's environment evolves through the interests and input of children. Role-modelling, working alongside the children, encourages them to pursue their interest. For example, Jagdeep (4 yrs) dug alongside adults every day when the sandpit was excavated. Children originally involved in creating the beach have left, but it still benefits existing children who continually contribute their ideas. Without following the children's interests, it would be sterile.

Observations inform practitioners when children are ready to communicate their knowledge, skills or expertise. They need input to gain language that will help

Image 2.2   Playing in the sandpit

them to think and describe. Practitioners who talk to children (even with no verbal response from children), impart essential grammatical structures and vocabulary. They empower them with vital words, with their interest's terminology, highlighting expertise.

> *Children admired William's (5 yrs) rolls down the mud slide. Lily (4½ yrs) was daring but frustrated with her attempts. She exclaimed 'I can't do it!' William explained incredibly accurately how to position her body. Lily followed his instructions, succeeding first time.*

Both exulted in her achievement and William was satisfied with his contribution, demonstrating that he could scaffold his learning (Bruce, 2001).

The practitioner's role is to offer an array of opportunities and experiences. Children exposed to them can discover their own interests, strengths and skills, becoming empowered and reflective in their learning.

The best description for practitioners is as *facilitators/motivators*. This is not passive: it demands imagination, creativity, deep knowledge of child development and how learning occurs. Facilitators are involved physically, intellectually, emotionally and socially. They sincerely respect children, have high aspirations and high expectations. Children are treated equally but not the same; are neither patronised nor underestimated. Inclusive provision is broad, natural and simple. The children's interests and contributions shape the setting.

Case study – Scarlet's well-being

Scarlet (3½ yrs) has problems interacting with children and adults, exhibiting low well-being. Adults know her love for outdoor space and her remarkable imagination: getting into character is real to her.

Once, she played with small-world animals, unusually indoors. The following day, acknowledging her preference, animals were set outside with natural resources. Scarlet headed for them, spending the session there. She created animated animal stories. Another child joined her, in parallel first, but quickly they communicated through storying.

The play soon extended to other children. She steadily started communicating more, marking the start of a calmer, happier Scarlet, more integrated and developing a sense of belonging. Her well-being increased and the outdoor small-world area became permanent. (Laevers et al., 2006)

Scarlet gained so much from this but also left a legacy for all: the area remains popular, eliciting fabulous imaginative play.

Outdoors, features gain character through the stimulus of individuals or groups, becoming truly powerful and awe-inspiring. This creates energy and motivates all children and adults. Providing for one child so often provides for all. The provision developed for/with one child opens opportunities for others; and in turn they influence it, multiplying opportunities.

Image 2.3   Small world

Planning for children's interests equates to personalised learning and effective differentiation. Children play and learn, whatever the provision – it is an inner driving force in the young of many species – but the quality of play and learning is dependent on the quality of the environment and the appropriateness of adult intervention (Curtis and Carter, 2003). Both require continual and relevant observations to enable adults to extend children's play hence their learning. When children initiate experiences, they are meaningful to them.

Principles into practice: what does this look like in practice?

When adults and environment promote well-being (Laevers et al., 2006), children pursue their interests, becoming deeply involved in their learning. The role of adults is to extricate the core of children's interests enabling them, through relevant provision and intervention, to broaden their interests, skills and knowledge.

Empathy, interest, professional training, calibre and imagination are prerequisites to understanding children's interests. Effective practitioners:

- respect children

- are deep listeners and keen observers

- understand pedagogy

- have high aspirations and high expectations

- use aspirational language

- endorse a positive learning culture

- are creative

- share children's joys and excitement.

They facilitate provision which is:

- practical, hands-on: outdoors is significant and unequivocal

- moral: outdoors is a natural backdrop to learning and consolidating values

- intellectual: outdoors presents a wealth of problem-solving opportunities pursuing interests in children's own time and pace

- emotional: children can connect with nature

- social: outdoors stimulates natural encounters, co-operation and respect for others' spaces and activity.

Practically, outdoors offers varied experiences, particularly effective on a large scale, such as running or building dens. Children can be active, whole bodied, messy, noisy, exuberant or quiet. Fresh air and natural scents stimulate calmness. Children's senses are invigorated exploring their surroundings; the weather adds another dimension.

Image 2.4   Playing in the mud

Children participate directly; learning is contextualised. It is first-hand, when nowa-days many children experience the world indirectly through IT and media.

> *Periodically, mud becomes dominant and adults must embrace this, for children to feel comfortable. Children create mud slides, often visited daily: sliding, rolling down and getting covered with it. It is exhilarating and perfect for children with trajectory or rotational schemas. A routine was quickly perfected to strip off muddy waterproofs with parents becoming used to muddy clothes.*

Morally, outdoors develops a sense of responsibility towards nature and its components, mineral, vegetable or animal. Continual access leads to close affinity and attachment.

 Case study – Harvey

Harvey (3½ yrs) had a speech impediment often frustrating him. Being outside released him, enabling him to explore gross and fine motor skills aiding speech development. He loved imaginative play and could, outside, engage in play not reliant on language but on action, communicating with others unworriedly, with enjoyment. He became unconsciously more engaged in talking parts. Outdoor imaginative play was his catalyst.

His interest in the natural world became dominant. His knowledge increased through questions, books and the internet.

Language no longer an issue, he acquired a phenomenal vocabulary. He transmitted interest and enthusiasm to others (for example in 30 minutes around a tree observing, describing insects to others and handling them sensitively). An expert, he oozed confidence.

Outdoors and adult support enabled Harvey to find his interest and aptitude, providing opportunities for others.

Nature is a positive influence on children's view of themselves and their place in the world.

> Alvaro (6 yrs) feels responsible towards the environment. He researched endangered species at home, particularly the plight of polar bears. He talked to adults about the need for action and humanity's role in this tragedy. He found that using electricity affects global warming, melting the ice essential to their survival. He took positive action, switching off lights and unused computers, telling people how many bears were saved through it.

Adults listened, took him seriously, encouraged his research and communicated with his mother.

Children have direct experience of the cycle of life, making death a part of it.

> Children spent time observing ants trying to move a dead beetle.

> Children observed a dead squirrel in detail. It prepared them for the death of their guinea pig shortly after.

Adults must be at ease with these aspects of natural life and transcend their own predispositions and anxieties to support children's learning. Effective adults are tolerant.

Outdoors proffers opportunities for independence and self-organisation. Children take responsibilities and make their own risk assessments.

> Offsite, in summer, nettles dominate some areas. Once, a child tripped, his arms falling into nettles. Logan (4 yrs) found him a dock leaf, then gave more to others as a preventative measure.

This child understands risk assessment and takes action, making an informed choice. Adults support this by thinking carefully about what safety implies, particularly in a world gone overboard with prevention. Children can only learn to make the right decision and assess risk by being confronted with it. The crux is to be as safe as necessary **not** as safe as possible, therefore not removing adventure (Lindon, 2003). We could have scythed the nettles, but this would not help children to deal with them nor the area's eco-system. Finding solutions rather than problems is vital for adults to support children's interests.

The emotional climate of the outdoors encourages children to express their feelings. It conveys a sense of freedom. Our brain relaxes: nowhere else can provide a substitute for this.

> As soon as they arrive at the setting, some children take shoes and socks off to go outside, needing direct contact with nature, wriggling their toes, feeling the ground and their faces conveying pleasure.

Some of these two-year-olds have problems interacting and communicating. Adults observed that with shoes off they are calmer, more tolerant and more likely to share. Direct contact with the earth seems to give them a firm foundation. Adults must accept such spontaneous behaviour even in colder weather: children **can** make their own decisions when it is too cold.

Children need to deal with their frustrations to maximise play opportunities, be receptive and become engaged in deep learning. Outdoors offers options,

Image 2.5   Barefoot in the water

being a backcloth where adults can support individuals in developing strategies (Bruce, 2001).

> *Ashton (3 yrs) is full-time; at some point daily he feels tetchy, reacting negatively to others. An adult takes him to the hammock under trees where they sit quietly. Minutes later, Ashton resumes his play re-energised. The next day, when becoming irascible, the hammock is suggested. Thereafter, at the onset of this feeling, Ashton takes himself to the hammock, sometimes enveloping himself, shutting out the world.*

Words were not applicable to find a solution. Ashton needed to establish a strategy to control his feelings. Handling emotions is life-long learning.

Outdoors, children build resilience. Their inborn curiosity is naturally stimulated and they develop interest through access.

> *During a June walk, Kavita (2½ yrs) wanted to pick unripe blackberries. An adult showed her the stages of growth. Each week, Kavita checked the berries. With adult encouragement she recorded and photographed her findings. In August, she was able to collect, eat them and make pies!*

Kavita learnt to be patient. The adult equipped her with a course of actions to support and scaffold her learning. Memorable teaching established memorable learning (Curtis and Carter, 2003).

Social involvement is inevitable outdoors. Outdoors offers real-life opportunities and need not be staged by practitioners. Adults' role is allowing this to flow, encouraging it by participating at children's level, continually observing to promote possibilities.

A favourite place offsite is a stream, where the banks can be slippery. Maya (3½ yrs) noticed another child struggling to climb out so she called, offering her hand. The practitioner's approval prompted her to continue with others who also modelled her behaviour. Children helped each other up and down.

This shows awareness, empathy and team spirit. Maya already understands that a team is the sum of its parts. With words of affirmation, the practitioner triggered others copying her.

Children become resourceful by learning in different ways, being analytical, experimenting and applying existing learning to new situations (Featherstone et al., 2008; Gardner, 1999).

Some children (3 to 8 yrs) became interested in conker pods on the ground. When opened they revealed immature conkers. Children, fascinated by their whiteness and size, began seeking the smallest conkers. Jack (7 yrs) found a piece of wood resembling a miniature pick-axe. He used it to prize pods open but struggled holding both conker and tool. He found a root with a concave curve fitting the pods' size and proceeded to open conkers.

Jack explained what he was doing. The adult suggested that it would be how the first tools were conceived. This generated a search for other ideas and an interest in tools in general. The quality of the questioning encouraged him to think about the process he had employed.

When supported, children are able to scaffold their own learning. This gives indications to adults about the next stage and/or extensions (Sutherland, 2008).

 Case study – Molly

Molly (5 yrs) shaped 'dinosaur eggs' with sand. An adult worked alongside. Molly talked about a dinosaur she 'saw' through the setting's window once and these were her eggs. Together, they found a safe place to store them. The practitioner bought bones from a pet shop, burying them in the garden. The next day, she told Molly that she had located traces of bones when planting. Excited, Molly went straight to the spot and dug. She analysed the bones and determined that they were 'definitely dinosaur bones'.

This engendered a lot more digging activities. With support Molly also researched dinosaurs, sharing her findings, and planned a museum and newspaper article. Knowing Molly's dominant connection schema, adults could instigate great interest from a very simple prompt.

Molly's skills and knowledge were reinforced and taken further. She was able to work independently and with others. She was stimulated and her learning encompassed all curriculum areas without being contrived. Using natural material, outdoors ensures that learning is meaningful, purposeful and memorable (Curtis and Carter, 2003).

Children become competent thinkers when they enjoy the adventure of learning by exploring freely a natural, stimulating and meaningful environment, by expressing their feelings and ideas to make sense of life and by acquiring a sense of belonging (Bruce, 2001). Outdoors with discerning adults offers a truly holistic and complete experience which values independence in thoughts and in actions and which meets children's interests.

Moving forwards

 Things to think about and do

Through an audit of practice and whole team discussion, review and evaluate how effective your outdoor provision is in these key areas.

- How proactive are adults outdoors in stimulating and supporting children's interests?
- How involved are the children in creating their outdoor play environment?
- How well are observations used to gain knowledge of children's interests and learning strategies and to plan for the next step?
- How well does the setting promote knowledge of useful pedagogical tools, such as documentation and knowledge of schema, through training?

 Key messages

- Outdoors, the freedom to be active on a large scale allows young children to engage in the way they most need to explore, make sense of life and express their feeling and ideas.
- Many young children relate much more strongly to learning offered outdoors.
- All areas of learning must be offered through a wide range of holistic experiences, both active and calm, which make the most of what the outdoors has to offer.
- Outdoor provision needs to be organised so that children are stimulated, and able, to follow their own interests and needs through play-based activity, giving them independence, self-organisation, participation and empowerment. The adult role is crucial in achieving this effectively.
- Appropriate outdoor provision promotes competent and confident learners.
- Children's ideas have to lead how the setting's environment is shaped, giving them ownership, making it real and alive.

Further reading and resources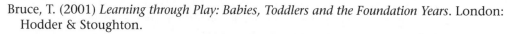

Bruce, T. (2001) *Learning through Play: Babies, Toddlers and the Foundation Years*. London: Hodder & Stoughton.

Featherstone, S. (ed.), Louis, S. Beswick, C. Magraw, L. and Hayes, L. (2008) *Again! Again! Understanding Schemas in Young Children*. London: A & C Black Publishing.

Sutherland, M. (2008) *Developing the Gifted and Talented Young Learner*. London: Sage.

Curtis, D. and Carter, M. (2003) *Designs for Living and Learning: Transforming Early Childhood Environments*. St Paul, MN: Redleaf Press.

Note

1 Schemas are themes of interest and behaviour that children focus on to find out about and understand the world around them. For more on schemas, see Featherstone et al. (2008) and Arnold (2010).

Adults are essential

The roles of adults outdoors

Tim Waller

This chapter explores:

- **Recent literature on the adult's role in outdoor play and learning**
- **The reasons why the adult's role is crucial**
- **The key aspects of the role**
- **Examples for discussion and reflection**

Value: Young children need all the adults around them to understand why outdoor play provision is essential for them, and adults who are committed and able to make its potential available to them.

Why are adults crucial for children's outdoor experiences?

Young children need practitioners who value and enjoy the outdoors themselves, see the potential and consequences it has for young children's well-being and development, and want to be outside with them. Attitude, understanding, commitment and positive thinking are important, as well as the skills to make the best use of what the outdoors has to offer and to effectively support child-led learning; the adult role outdoors must be as deeply considered as that indoors. Practitioners must be able to recognise, capture and share children's learning outdoors with parents and other people working with the child, so that they too become enthused. Cultural differences in attitude to the outdoors need to be understood and worked with sensitively to reach the best outcomes for children.

The attitude, role and behaviour of adults is fundamental and absolutely crucial for children to be able engage in regular and appropriate experience of a range of outdoor spaces from birth onwards. Opportunities to play outdoors every day, to engage with the environment in all weather conditions and to build an understanding and appreciation of the natural world are experiences which all young children are entitled to (Sustainable Development Commission, 2007) and these opportunities will not be available without adult involvement and support.

Firstly and foremost, enthusiastic adults help to foster positive dispositions towards outdoor environments which may become enduring habits of mind and last for life (Muñoz, 2009). The *Early Years Foundation Stage Effective Practice: Outdoor Learning* (DCSF 2008c: 2) establishes this principle from the outset:

> The attitude and behaviour of adults outdoors has a profound impact on what happens there and on children's learning. It is therefore vital that children have the support of attentive and engaged adults who are enthusiastic about the outdoors and understand the importance of outdoor learning.

Waite, Davis and Brown (2006: 59) note that 'This enthusiasm is underpinned by a firm conviction in *the value of outdoor learning*' (emphasis in original). They argue that adults' 'belief in its value is further demonstrated by their persistence and *willingness to overcome obstacles*, such that any barriers are addressed to ensure access for children to the outdoors'.

There are many potential barriers for adults facilitating or engaging in outdoor activity with children and young people (Ouvry, 2003). Opportunities for outdoor play have become much more restricted over the last three generations due to a rise in traffic, the greater institutionalisation of childhood (breakfast and after school clubs, etc.) and parents' safety concerns (Holloway and Valentine, 2000). For Muñoz (2009: 17), parental perceptions and fears relating to outdoor spaces play a major role in determining children's ability to use outdoor spaces. Parents and practitioners are therefore the 'gatekeepers' to children's levels of access and experience outdoors.

Access

Adult attitudes to outdoor play have been highlighted as one of the main factors in determining children's access (Waite et al., 2006). Early years practitioners need to understand and recognise the significant potential of outdoor learning and, in addition to developing outside play opportunities within their grounds, they should also consider giving children regular opportunities to experience wild natural environments (Waller, 2009).

In both these contexts it appears that practitioners' attitudes and dispositions towards the shared construction of learning are key factors. The outdoor environment should be viewed as a place that offers a range of distinctly unique opportunities and potential for play and learning (White, 2008) rather than being purely a set of physical features.

Access to outdoor environments also involves giving children opportunity for appropriate physical challenges to support and facilitate their emotional development, especially confidence, resilience and self-esteem, and overall strength, coordination and gross motor skills (Ouvry, 2003). Children naturally and regularly seek out and enjoy physical challenges in their play, as a matter of course. We have to consider the negative consequences if children do not confront and conquer risky physical activities. Children therefore need the opportunity to take acceptable risks,

Image 3.1   In this photograph Harry (aged 2 yrs 3 mths) is accompanied by his grandparents to a local park. In the picture his grandfather supports Harry's desire to climb up the wooden frame. Note his concentration and disposition, how the adult is in close proximity to Harry but allows him to take appropriate risks, and the opportunity to demonstrate confidence and competence.

and the question for adults is how to juggle the requirement for safety with the need for children to have physical challenges, as illustrated in Image 3.1 (see also Tovey, 2007, Chapter 8 and the case study Children aged 2–3 years in this chapter).

Ofsted (2006) have identified good practice in terms of health and safety in early years settings. This guidance does **not** suggest risk and challenge are removed from young children's experience. It highlights examples where children undertake 'risky' behaviour in a 'controlled and supportive' environment. For example, 'a child using a rake was given help to use it safely without his fun being spoilt' (2006: 10). This report identified that the main strategy in settings that were particularly effective at keeping children safe was that adults emphasised helping children *learn how* to keep themselves safe.

Giving children access to a range of outdoor experiences is clearly important, but their disposition to enjoy and learn outside is strongly influenced by adult behaviour. For example, I recently visited a number of settings during a period of heavy snowfall, for another research project. Some settings were closed and in the ones that were open, no children were outside at any period. The reason given was that it was 'too cold'. Yet many of the children who were not at school because it was closed were taken out to play in the snow by their parents. Only appropriate clothing was needed – the children were clearly keen to play in the snow. This example provides an interesting contrast to Scandinavian settings that put babies outside in prams (suitably wrapped up and under cover) in temperatures well below zero.

If adult dispositions are that they don't go outside in the rain or the cold, then children will learn these dispositions too. One interesting effect of the Outdoor Learning Project (OLP – see below and Waller, 2009) is that, as a result of their regular visits to the Country Park in all weathers, children are observed to choose to play outside more regularly at Nursery in all types of weather. Thus knowledgeable and enthusiastic adults are crucial to unlocking the potential of outdoors, as are their attitudes and dispositions.

What is the adult's role in supporting children's outdoor play and learning?

The role of early years practitioners in outdoor environments is both complex and multiple and Casey (2007) suggests that the free-flowing playground situation may present a particular challenge. Some practitioners define their role as mainly interactive indoors and more monitorial outdoors and there has also been some recent debate about what we mean by learning outdoors being a 'seamless' experience from learning inside. Edgington (2002) contends that the space, size and features of outdoor environments necessarily changes the sort of learning experiences children may have. It could also be argued that part of the attraction of the outdoors is as a contrasting experience to the traditional and formal modes of learning more commonly found in classrooms (White, 2008).

There is a long history of outdoor provision in early years education and care in the UK (Garrick, 2009) which has recently been influenced and supplemented by outdoor education traditions from Scandinavia and the approach to learning in Reggio Emilia, Italy (Waller, 2009). There is therefore a clear message from past and recent research and literature about the nature and function of the adult's role in supporting children's outdoor play and learning. In this role, staff are reflective practitioners, thinkers, researchers and co-constructors of knowledge with children (Waller, 2007). Key aspects of this role, which relate to children of all ages, include:

- developing (outdoor) relationships with children and facilitating communication

- entering children's worlds, identifying and building on children's outdoor interests, scaffolding play and sustained shared thinking

- providing opportunities for child-initiated play and outdoor play free from an adult's gaze

- helping children negotiate and maintain play and modelling inclusive behaviour

- supporting appropriate challenging and risky play

- teaching children about the natural world and care of the environment

- providing opportunities for outdoor play in varied physical environments including wild 'natural' areas on a regular basis

- working with parents and carers as well as children in outdoor spaces (see the case study Children under 12 months in this chapter).

Relationships and interaction

The relationships and interaction between children and adults are the most important aspect of promoting effective outdoor play. Outdoor environments afford opportunities for a balance between adult-led structured activities and giving children access to interesting outdoor spaces with some private space free from adult intrusion (Cullen, 1993). For Ouvry (2003), participation in children's spontaneous play, talk and exploration is what should take up most of a practitioner's time outside (see Image 3.2). Roberts (2010: 105), writing about children's well-being from birth, argues that 'tuning-in' to children's play, as shown in Image 3.2, involves 'sensitive companions [who] understand that the starting points for children's play need to be anchored in children's own interests and experiences'. This involves 'letting go' and giving children authority in their own play (see Waller, 2007).

Recently in the UK, longitudinal research in early years settings has identified strong evidence for the value of adults engaging with children collaboratively

Image 3.2   In a nursery school garden a child (aged 3 yrs 6 mths) invites a nursery assistant to join in her play.

in activity through the strategy of 'sustained shared thinking' to support their cognitive development (e.g. Siraj-Blatchford et al., 2002). It is possible that the space and time afforded in large outside spaces provides greater opportunity for sustained shared thinking than inside the classroom (Waller, 2007) and also unique and unexpected occasions for authentic learning (see Image 3.3). For Waite et al. (2006: 59), 'Achieving a delicate balance of intervention is perhaps even more crucial in a freer outside environment requiring staff to show considerable *sensitivity to the appropriateness of free and structured activity* at different points in children's play and learning' (emphasis in original).

Children's voice and child initiated learning outside

Waite et al. (2006) make the case that another very important aspect of the adult role is the need to consider the involvement of children in planning and use of outdoors. They argue that this approach seemed to ensure a greater sense of ownership, more engagement and higher levels of usage. As Tovey (2007) points out, time and care should be taken to set up resources with the children and the Every Child Matters Outcomes Framework (DCSF, 2008a: 3) recommends 'the priority given to specific types of experiences needs ongoing review and adaptation to reflect the changing interests and enthusiasms of the children currently using the outdoor space' (see the case study Children aged 5–7 years in this chapter).

In Waller (2007, 2009) I report on an example of child-initiated outdoor learning with children aged 3–5 years. In this Outdoor Learning Project the children developed enduring shared narratives around the specific locations in the outdoor spaces, supported and enhanced by the adults as co-constructors. I describe in particular the benefits for the participating children and adults in documenting their experiences through 'learning stories' (Carr, 2001). The narratives frequently include the interactions between teacher and learner, or between peers; often the episode is dictated by the learner as a 'child's voice'. Here learning processes are documented in various ways so that they can be shared, discussed, reflected upon, interpreted and developed.

As children become older (and particularly from five years on), outdoor environments may support increased opportunities to develop resilience, friendships and self-determination because adult influence is reduced and children co-operate (Waite et al., 2006). Corsaro (2005) suggests that children's independence is fostered by lower levels of adult control often observed in outdoor contexts.

Children's appreciation and understanding of the natural environment

Ouvry (2003) encourages staff to interact with children outside, not as supervisors but as educators, and views the outdoor space as an essential teaching area. A key aspect of teaching children outdoors relates to the need to promote children's appreciation and understanding of the natural environment. Simply giving children opportunities to be outdoors may not be sufficient for them to learn about nature and to care for the natural would – it is the role of significant adults in the lives of young people to impart ethical concerns and enhance a relationship with nature (Muñoz, 2009). Further, for Muñoz (2009) children will only gain this understanding if they become a specific focus of teaching. Outside, there are endless opportunities for children and adults to grow plants, vegetables, etc. and observe, record and document bird and animal life *together*. The Early Years Foundation Stage Effective Practice guidance states that:

> It is important to help children to care for the environment by helping them to understand the need to take litter away with them, not to damage or remove plants or trees or wildlife and to respect other people's rights to enjoy the space as well. When children are encouraged to use the open spaces in the locality they can be helped to respect the environment and to feel a sense of ownership and pride in it. (DCSF, 2008c: 4)

Image 3.3 4-year-olds attending a Nursery School in England are taken on regular visits to a local country park.

Julie, Julie, come over here quick – there's something moving!

I've caught it – what is it?

It's a newt.

What's that?

Can we take it back to nursery with us?

Case study – Children under 12 months

Practitioners working at a Sure Start Children's Centre attended a course on outdoor learning at a local university. Consequently, they were keen to learn more about Scandinavian approaches to outdoor provision and the university tutor helped them make contact with a setting in Stavanger, Norway, and an exchange was arranged. On their return to the UK, staff were keen to develop their outdoor provision and in particular give the children access to the outdoors every day, in all weathers. This included daytime sleeping arrangements where the children under 12 months were placed in prams under a veranda, wrapped in blankets and appropriate clothing. Staff were convinced that the children would benefit from regular exposure to fresh air and this would enhance their immune system and physical well-being. However, some parents, including those whose heritage and cultural background was from warmer climates, objected to their children being placed outside in the winter months.

Questions to explore

1 How might practitioners resolve the parents' concerns?

2 What is the research evidence for the benefits of regular fresh air at an early age?

3 Can outdoor cultural traditions from Scandinavia be easily replicated in the UK?

 Case study – Children aged 2–3 years

Rory (aged 2 yrs, 3 mths) attended his local village playgroup every morning, which is staffed by experienced, well qualified practitioners. The playgroup is located in the village hall in a large room which has multiple use. There is access to a tarmac outside area which is adjacent to the car park. However, staff understood that it is necessary to give children access to a broader range of outdoor experiences, which is also required in the Early Years Foundation Stage (DCSF, 2008b). They arranged for the children to be taken regularly on foot in small groups to the local park where there is also a possibility of play and exploration in a small wooded area, accompanied by one member of staff along with a rota of parents and community members. Rory was particularly keen to climb on fixed apparatus and trees. He appeared to be very strong and well coordinated for his age and according to his mother is very active, taking up every opportunity to play outside. In the park Rory was easily able to climb his age-designated fixed apparatus and was supported by adults to climb on other apparatus. He appeared determined to climb well above his own height in trees in the wood.

Questions to explore

1 How should practitioners best support Rory's desire to climb higher?

2 How do children benefit from climbing?

3 What are appropriate risk assessments for climbing trees?

Case study – Children aged 5–7 years

An inner-city infant school is located in a Victorian building and has a traditional rectangular playground, which is small for 220 children. At break and lunchtime this playground appeared dominated by a group of older boys playing football, with all other children tending to play around the periphery. Staff became concerned about the aggressive behaviour of some children and the general range of outdoor facilities in the school. Over a period of time, they decided to make changes to the outdoor provision and, after consulting all staff, parents and children, they made the following amendments:

- break times were staggered to allow for a smaller group of children to use the space

- staff introduced a range of traditional singing and skipping games which quickly became popular with the children

- after consultation with the adjacent junior school, they arranged to use their larger playground for football and ball games

- after researching the local area, the staff and governors persuaded the local authority to allow them access to a piece of land opposite the school which had been left to grow wild and included a pond. Small groups of children accompanied by staff visit regularly in break and teaching times

- the Local Authority regularly provides a bus to transport children to out-of-school activities. Previously, these visits were mainly to museums and art galleries but the list of venues for these visits was adapted to include a local hillside woodland owned by the National Trust. Staff arranged for the Forest Rangers to meet children in this location on a regular basis.

Questions to explore

1 What is the most important factor necessary to make the above changes?

2 How might the children benefit from changes to outdoor provision?

3 What are the links between informal learning outside and more formal teaching inside?

Moving forwards

 ## Things to think about and do

- Reflect on your own practice and audit your current outdoor provision in the setting (see Casey, 2007).

- Where possible arrange to visit outdoor provision in other settings (consult with your Local Authority advisers).

- Explore your locality to determine appropriate 'wild' outdoor spaces to visit on foot.

(Continued)

(Continued)

- Elicit the help of parents, members of the community and students to support regular outdoor visits.
- Contact your local Forest Rangers and nearest Forest School.

Key messages

- Apart from the natural environment, adults are the most valuable resource for outdoor play and learning.
- The only other essential resource is appropriate clothing that enables children and adults to be outside in all weathers (settings may need to consider providing this).
- The role of the adult in outside environments is to sensitively support children's play and ideas and give them the opportunity for private space and time for exploration.
- Children need access to a wide range of outdoor experiences both in the setting and in wild 'natural' environments.
- The range and priority given to outdoor provision needs ongoing review and adaptation to reflect the changing interests and enthusiasms of the children.
- Children need to be specifically taught about the natural environment, conservation and sustainability.
- Practitioners need to consider providing an environment that is both safe and one where children feel secure enough to take appropriate risks.
- Regular engagement in outdoor activities is beneficial and enjoyable for both the children and staff involved.

Further reading and resources

Wilson, R. (2008) *Nature and Young Children: Encouraging Creative Play and Learning in Natural Environments*. London and New York: David Fulton.

Garrick, R. (2009) *Playing Outdoors in the Early Years* (2nd edn). London, New York: Continuum.

Perry, J.P. (2001) *Outdoor Play: Teaching Strategies with Young Children*. New York: Teachers College Press.

Taking Learning Outdoors: www.LTScotland.org.uk/learningteachingandassessment/approaches/outdoorlearning

Learning through Landscapes: http://www.ltl.org.uk/

Forest Schools in the UK: http://www.forestschools.com/index.php and www.foresteducation.org

Capturing the difference

The special nature of the outdoors

Jan White

> **This chapter explores:**
>
> - **Why the special nature of the outdoor environment must be the focus for outdoor provision and planning**
> - **What is different and unique about the outdoor environment and being outdoors for young children's exploration, play, learning and development**
> - **What providers can do to harness these special characteristics for children's play**
>
> *Value: The outdoor space and curriculum must harness the special nature of the outdoors, to offer children what the indoors cannot. This should be the focus for outdoor provision, complementing and extending provision indoors.*

Why is it important to focus on the special nature of the outdoors?

Remember a favourite place for play outside from your childhood: what made it a good place? What did it feel like? What did it have in it? What could you do there? If you recall your own play as a child, play outside probably had a very different flavour to that indoors. The play spaces outside are likely to have been quite different to favourite indoor spaces and to have had certain characteristics that made them good physical, emotional and social places for being, playing and developing in.

The everyday experience of practitioners that being outdoors is very important to young children is consistently endorsed by research studies (e.g. Clark and Moss, 2001). The outdoors is different to the indoors and being outdoors is different to being indoors: this is why it matters. In order to provide rich and satisfying outdoor play for children from birth to five and beyond, it is vital to consider what it is that being outdoors offers them. Why do they like the outdoors? Why is it a good learning environment for them? How does it add to the provision possible indoors?

Unpicking what makes it different to being indoors ensures that the outdoor play we provide will capture this difference. Rather than attempting to 'take the indoors out', it is vital to capture the special nature of the outdoors to offer children what the indoors cannot. If we don't harness this potential, we are missing the point – and missing the huge capacity of the outdoors to help young children thrive and grow, adding greatly to what the indoors can offer.

> Being outdoors, potentially, exposes children to a range of experiences and opportunities which cannot be replicated inside a building, however well it is designed and equipped. (Wendy Titman, 2009)

The outdoors is a vital, special and deeply engaging place for children. It feels very different and allows the child to be different. It offers a climate, culture and opportunities that are just not available inside. The outdoors provides children with essential experiences vital to their well-being, health and development and offers different ways of behaving, relating and interacting. Often, these experiences tap into deep natural motivations that are highly holistic, supporting the child's inner and outer life as a whole.

This chapter explores how the outdoors is different and what it can provide that the indoors does not. Practitioners must have a deep belief, and a strong rationale to share with parents, that outdoor provision is vital for all children, from birth onwards. Providers must be very clear about *why* children should learn outdoors as well as indoors, and able to articulate this to others so that they become convinced too. Such analysis also gives a clear guide as to just *what* it is that providers should be seeking to harness in what they offer and how they manage provision outdoors. Once we know what it is that we should be capturing, we can think about how well that is actually happening and what can be done to make these special characteristics fully present in our outdoor provision.

The outdoors is a precious resource for well-being and learning that is both significantly different from *and* complementary to the indoors. Our focus must be on what the outdoors is able to provide that makes it valuable, important and necessary in every early years setting.

What makes the outdoors different?

What does the outdoors offer that indoors cannot? What are the features of the outdoors that cannot be offered on the same scale or the same way indoors? How can these special characteristics be captured in early years outdoor spaces?

Space and scale

On moving from inside to the outdoors we are struck by the wide range of sensations on both body and mind that the much larger space gives. The dimension of 'up' also becomes much more apparent and young children love to be up high, gaining new perspectives and looking down on others. The space outdoors *feels* very different: it is a different mental and emotional space, which makes us feel quite different to how we felt indoors.

A good outdoor environment encourages children to work on a larger, more active scale and to play in larger groups, but also provides a variety of spaces and places allowing children to move between large and small scale play and to choose activity and interaction levels. Space itself has a significant impact on young children, and each of these spaces gives its own sensations and messages about how to feel and what to do. Young children, especially toddlers, are drawn to the miniscule, and the outdoors has a great deal to offer here too. It is important that adults tune into, value and join in with children's fascination with the tiny side of the world.

Freedom

Being able to do things not possible indoors is a crucial part of the rationale for outdoor play and deciding what it should provide. The outdoors offers children many freedoms that both extend what they are able to do indoors and make possible experiences that are very different. Sand, water play and gardening are aspects of provision that work especially well outdoors. Children have room and permission to be energetic, boisterous and exuberant, and to engage in their strong desires to transport and mix materials, while feeling uninhibited about action, noise, dirt, spillage and mess, releasing them from the constraints that their way of learning necessitates indoors.

Outdoors, children can be more relaxed, inventive and adventurous – with ideas as well as with their body. They often experience more freedom to initiate their play and follow their own ideas, and they can manipulate and create their own play environments. Above all, perhaps, young children can experience the freedoms of being themselves and of exploring different ways of being, feeling, behaving and interacting – from cloud-watching to superhero play.

Fresh air and being active

Just being outside has wide-ranging effects on physical and mental well-being. Cool, moving, oxygen-rich air is refreshing and enlivening. Since sunlight maintains good sleep and immune system function, helps us to be alert and ready to learn, and stimulates production of vitamin D and the 'happiness' brain chemical serotonin, it is vital that children are bathed in natural light throughout the year.

Being active builds bones, body tissue, neurological systems and brain connections, and also helps children to eat and sleep well. Movement and action develops vision, balance, body awareness, coordination, functioning, organisation and regulation in the brain and body (Goddard Blythe, 2008). Young children are naturally active in short bursts, so ongoing access to the outdoor environment significantly raises activity and fitness levels (Doherty and Whiting, 2004).

Many children are clearly much happier when they are free to move, and when children's movement needs are met, behaviour issues tend to disappear. Children need to derive pleasure from the feelings of their bodies in action – feeling good

Image 4.1   Whole-bodied learning – the lighthouse-keeper's lunch

in and about your body is the foundation for an emotionally and physically healthy life.

Movement

The biological drive to move is very strong indeed: for example, toddlers learning to walk can take up to 9,000 walking steps in a day (Adolph et al., 2003)! Through movement children are developing several fundamental neurological systems (Stock Kranowitz, 2005), and opportunity for movement is an important special feature of any outdoor environment. Thoughtful practitioners can do much to make this happen through the culture, environment, resources and experiences they provide.

Children must be physical on both large and small scales, enjoy a wide range of playful physical activities and have movement integrated into as many experiences as possible. Children working on locomotion and coordination from birth onwards need unobstructed open space, pathways to travel along and a variety of surfaces demanding a range of attention, effort and body control, such as grass, paving, sand, gravel, bark, packed earth and decking. They need uneven and less predictable surfaces; surfaces that 'give' underfoot; sloping, bumpy and hilly surfaces; surfaces with a variety of levels; and they need to clamber and master the art of going up and down slopes and steps.

Embodied learning

Alongside this support for physicality, is the wonderful way the outdoors involves the whole child at a deep level in every experience. The types of materials and resources, and the ways and scale on which they can be used, enables the child to use their whole self in whatever they do. This whole-body, multi-sensory, active learning-by-moving-and-doing fits very strongly with the way young children learn best (Medina, 2008).

These deeper experiences make more 'sense' and are more memorable, giving embodied 'felt meanings' that underpin more abstract thinking later on. Exploration and play in a large sand area and with running water give deeply felt meanings of volume, weight, distance and height that will later be used in mathematical and scientific thinking. We think in all the ways we experience (Robinson and Aronica, 2009): the more active the child can be and the more parts of their body they can use at once, the better the child understands and learns. So practitioners must plan for experiences that enable children to move and be hands-on, and look for ways to extend activities for whole-body involvement.

Real experiences

A rich learning environment bathes children in direct, hands-on experience of the real physical world and the real lives of humans. Children need personal contact with the real stuff of the world before it can become the material for rich and satisfying play. The outdoors is amazingly rich in possibilities for motivational real-world and first-hand experiences, even in a small outdoor area. In particular, these can come from nature, the weather, the seasons, gardening and growing, the locality and community, being adventurous, dealing with challenge and learning how to keep safe. Every season brings different and intriguing conditions in the weather, features in the natural world, ways of feeling, things to deal with, and possibilities for exploring and playing.

Young children also revel in being involved in the real tasks that adults do, being included in the daily life and care of their own environment by helping to set out, tidy up, clean resources and care for plants and animals. These kinds of activities are full of learning potential in all domains, and result in a strong sense of belonging.

Stimulus and possibility

Every outdoor space has a vast array of stimuli for babies, toddlers and young children, with so much to engender curiosity and fascination. Children notice things about the outdoor environment with the perspective of, 'what can I do here?' or, 'what can I do with this?' For example, steps might be used to climb up, balance along and jump from, bounce a ball down, lie along on their tummy, look out from, sit on with a friend or make into a pretend house. Such a feature has high play value for children, but its potential 'affordance' (Brown, 2003) will be lost if the value of what they are doing is not well understood by adults.

Children look much more 'close-up' than adults do. They draw us in to watch ants, enjoy the delicate detail of moss, notice rain water running into the drain and

Image 4.2   A toddler delights in the way the wind moves the light material

marvel with them at the iridescent colours in a puddle. When this inborn sense of wonder is sustained, children thrive. We must capture these possibilities for deep involvement (Laevers et al., 2006), sustained shared thinking (Siraj-Blatchford et al., 2002) and feelings of shared pleasure (Carson, 1998).

Sensorial richness

The outdoors offers an extremely rich environment for all senses, including the 'kinaesthetic' (body) sense. For example, outdoors provides a world of sounds, where children can learn to hear them separately (discrimination), understand what they mean (recognition), work out where they are coming from (direction) and how far away they are (distance). Children with sensory impairments are well supported where information can be provided in a multi-dimensional way.

The outdoors has huge power in this area, especially when it has sand, water, grass, wood, stone, vegetation and other natural materials. Layers of sensorial richness are provided through:

- offering materials and resources to see, touch, hear, smell, taste, handle and move – playing in the rain and growing in real soil are just two of the very many possibilities

- creating a range of sensations through planting and surfaces that give different sensations

- making the boundaries of the outdoor space open enough so that the world beyond adds another layer of sensory richness.

Variety, change and spontaneity

The outdoors also has the capacity to provide huge variety and diversity. The human mind constantly looks for new stimulation and variation is what makes life interesting. Good outdoor environments offer a variety of spaces, big and small; a range of perspectives, from enclosed to open vistas; variation in surfaces, pathways, levels and gradients; and different materials to explore and transform, such as sand, soil and water.

Every day outdoors is different and offers so much for free! Daily variety in the quality of the air, temperature and rainfall, gradual changes through the seasons and how these affect things in the environment all bring huge potential for discovery and learning.

The outdoor world is a dynamic place, where change, chance, serendipity, spontaneity, surprise and excitement are constantly available, especially with adults who are ready to respond to opportunity. Occasional changes in routines, such as having snacktime under a big umbrella in the rain, offer further variety. The more children are outdoors, the better they are able to take full advantage of this endless variety and change.

Nature and natural elements

Children need nature in their environment, with personal 'everyday' contact with plants, mini-beasts, animals, sand, soil, natural materials, rain, sun, wind and ice (Warden, 2007; White, 2008). Much recent research indicates that nature plays a role in reducing life stress and increasing resilience (Parsons, 2007). Its presence makes the environment richer, softer, more dynamic and open to serendipity, offering complexity in a way that does not overwhelm.

Nature also strongly supports play (White, 2008). Water and sand are particularly important natural elements to provide and use in the widest way. Plants can provide both places for children to play amongst and superb play props to collect, organise and use in imaginative and creative play. A great deal is also gained from growing and taking care of plants together, especially when these become part of the play environment. Care for nature helps lay the foundations for empathy, responsibility and care for others. The pleasure, joy, awe and wonder available through contact with the natural world have a very powerful role in generating feelings of connectedness and well-being (Carson, 1998).

Play materials

Outdoors, children can access materials that support the way they learn best. Versatile, open-ended resources offer an enormous range of possibilities for play,

Image 4.3   Rich outdoor play provides personal 'everyday' contact with nature

can be used differently by every child and can be mentally transformed into anything the child wants them to be, developing symbolic thinking (Medina, 2008). Materials that can be physically transformed by combining or mixing make for especially fascinating and productive play. When materials can be collected, handled, manipulated and moved around, their play value is further enhanced, allowing children to mould and create their play environment. Use of the hands is a significant driver for brain development (Wilson, 1998), and 'loose parts' are a 'formidable ingredient for enabling children to engage in play' (Hughes, quoted in Brown and Taylor, 2008: 44).

This plasticity and affordance for child-led play results in high levels of motivation, involvement and inventiveness, complex social interaction, friendship, and sustained, meaningful play themes (Broadhead, 2003). Flexibility in the play environment leads to increased flexibility and innovation in the way the child plays (Brown, 2003), and children become architects and authors (Tovey, 2007: 55), building their own play, learning and 'self'.

Following their own interests

The wonderful combination of the real world, nature and versatile materials in a flexible space creates a highly enabling environment full of provocation and inspiration for creative and critical thinking. Young children are curious, exploratory, playful and self-driven learners, and outdoors they are stimulated to raise and solve a multitude of mathematical, scientific and imaginative problems with the freedom to pursue their own drives and interests. Children's ideas are often far more interesting than adults': practitioners who are confident outdoors and comfortable with the unexpected can find this to be a particularly rewarding aspect of their work.

The more flexible, action-oriented and child-led outdoor environment is especially good at enabling young children to pursue schematic interests, especially at the sensory-motor and functional dependency (cause and effect) stages. Schemas represent big questions and ideas and play a very significant role in developing thinking and learning (Arnold, 2010). It is important that adults are keen observers of schemas in play outdoors, so that they can help children to harness its great potential to broaden and deepen their enquiries.

Relationships

There is a different quality to the relationships a child can have outside with other children and with adults. There is time and space for being together and doing together, for companionship and conversation, and perhaps opportunity to be with younger and older children. Children who are more in their 'element' outside find it easier to relate to others, resulting in more communication of higher quality (Chilvers, 2006). Research shows that young boys build friendships through running, chasing and superhero play (Brown, 2009). The outdoors is special to children because it is more *their* place (Perry, 2001). Children may feel calmer, less controlled and less inhibited, perhaps experiencing the outdoors as a more equal and democratic place. Boys can find more meaning and motivation in things that they tend to avoid indoors, such as mark-making and problem-solving. Adults too can feel less disturbed by noise, movement and mess outside, and this might be important for how they view and relate to some individuals, particularly boisterous boys (Kindlon and Thompson, 2000).

 Case study – Sandfield Natural Play Centre

Sandfield is a private setting for children from birth to 11 in the north-west of England with a vision of offering all children 'curiosity, discovery, wonder, adventure, challenge and a strong sense of belonging'. It has a walled garden housing a 'play garden' for babies and toddlers and a 'forest garden' and 'growing garden' for older children, although all ages use both gardens, especially to be with siblings. It also has an adjoining woodland for journeys and adventures.

Because of good transition areas, children move between outdoors and indoors whenever they wish. Young children sleep outside and older ones can find many places there for softness, rest and refuge. There is a strong focus on open-ended, transformable materials, especially sand, soil, water and plants.

The team has taken time to develop a shared vision that focuses on the vital and special nature of the outdoors, especially the natural environment, and each child's own 'natural curriculum'. Staff and parents are rapidly developing their understanding of children's natural play behaviours, particularly through the use of 'learning stories', and witness daily how being outdoors inspires children's action and thinking, supports their happiness and health and encourages both adults and children to take their time and enjoy just being together.

What does this mean in practice?

The outdoors really is a fantastic place for young children's well-being and learning and can be a highly enabling and motivational environment. The key question that practitioners must ask themselves, as a team, is 'Are we making good use of the special things that outdoors offers children that the indoors does not?' In order to capture and harness this special nature, thinking, discussion and action at several levels are required.

- *The vision.* The setting needs to develop a strong, shared understanding and rationale, and a clear sense of purpose for its outdoor provision. This will set the direction for planning experiences and for any developments in provision and practice.

- *The environment.* The outdoor space (and beyond) should become a major part of the overall learning environment, being accessible and well used every day throughout the year, and the transition between inside and outside needs to work well. It must be easy to use and comfortable for both children and adults, with practical issues such as clothing, changing, toilets, shade, cover and wind protection addressed. Storage and organisation should make resources highly visible, very accessible and mobile. The most effective outdoor environment is diverse, flexible, open-ended and filled with nature and natural elements, especially sand, soil and water. A running water supply is essential.

- *Resources.* Build up abundant supplies of simple, open-ended, versatile and moveable resources, ensuring children learn how to use them successfully and safely. Children should then be supported to make their own choices about where and what to play, and to select and replace resources easily and independently from a consistently well-organised, tidy and continuously available bank.

- *Planning.* In order to capitalise upon what the outdoors has the potential to offer, a planning system that is flexible and responsive is necessary, enabling practitioners to both capture what is expected *and* respond to chance and opportunity. It is important to work with the weather, to use what is available and not to try to do things that are not effective in the current conditions.

- *Children.* To harness the child-led nature of play and learning outdoors, children need appropriate clothing, uncluttered space and plenty of open-ended, unstructured time. Their behaviour and actions must be well understood and supported, and they need to be viewed and treated as competent, trusted and responsible.

- *Adults.* Adults give children strong messages when they value the outdoors as a learning environment and fully appreciate the way young children learn best. Practitioners must be clothed so they can properly engage with activity and play. They need to be able to connect into children's interests and natural learning strategies and able to enjoy the unpredictability of being outside with young children. They must become confident, tuned-in and comfortable so that they can role-model curiosity, enquiry, playfulness and a positive approach to challenge.

Moving forwards

 Things to think about and do

- Ask staff to share memories of their favourite childhood play outdoors and to draw out what the special features of the play and the place were. This can be used as a starting point for thinking about things that are special about the outdoors for young children's experience and play.

- Using this chapter and your own analysis, observe and discuss what goes on in your current space to audit how well different aspects of the special nature of the outdoors are being captured at the moment.

- Consider what could be done in provision and/or practice to capture some more of the special nature of the outdoors. Don't forget to consider how you could make more of what you have already.

- Compile a shared list of what you as a team feel is special about the outdoors and explain these to parents. Have discussions with them too, so that their thoughts can be added and they become engaged with what you are seeking to do.

- Create a display of children accessing the special nature of the outdoors – ask the children to take photos of what is special for them for this display. Through discussions with the children you will be able to record and present their comments alongside.

- Develop a policy statement (rationale and vision) regarding making good use of what is special and unique about the outdoors as a driver for the setting's approach to outdoor play, and how this difference will be used to enhance children's experiences.

- Select one or two of the characteristics of the special nature of the outdoors that are particularly important in the ethos or purpose of your setting, and work to enhance how well they are captured in practice.

Key messages

- The outdoors offers young children essential experiences vital to their well-being, health and development in all areas. Children who miss these experiences are significantly deprived.

- Outdoors, children can have the freedom to explore different ways of 'being', feeling, behaving and interacting; they have space – physical (up as well as sideways), mental and emotional; they have room and permission to be active, interactive, messy, noisy and work on a large scale; they may feel less controlled by adults.

- The real contact with the elements, seasons and the natural world, the range of perspectives, sensations and environments – multi-dimensional and multi-sensory – and the daily change, uncertainty, surprise and excitement all contribute to the desire young children have to be outside. It cannot be the same indoors; a child cannot *be* the same indoors – outdoors is a vital, special and deeply engaging place for young children.

Further reading and resources

White, J. (2008) *Playing and Learning Outdoors: Making Provision for High Quality Experiences in the Outdoor Environment.* Abingdon: Routledge.

Warden, C. (2007) *Nurture through Nature.* Auchterader: Mindstretchers.

Babies Outdoors, Toddlers Outdoors, Two Year Olds Outdoors, DVDs and supporting notes, Siren Films with Jan White (Siren Films, 2010): www.sirenfilms.co.uk

The Mud Centre: Recapturing Childhood, by B.J. Jensen and J.A. Bullard Available at: www.communityplaythings.com/resources/articles/dramaticplay/mudcenter.html

5

A responsive environment

Creating a dynamic, versatile and flexible environment

Ros Garrick

This chapter explores:

- **The outdoors as a uniquely responsive environment, and one with the potential to promote young children's agency, to foster creativity and to strengthen dispositions for learning**
- **The principle of responsive environments in early childhood education and care**
- **How the principle can be realised in practice with babies and toddlers, young children, and children in the early school years**
- **How settings can move forward from varying starting points to create or enhance outdoor environments that are dynamic, versatile and flexible**

Value: Outdoors should be a dynamic, flexible and versatile place where children can choose, create, change and be in charge of their play environment.

The rationale for a responsive environment

Looking back to the 18th and 19th-century roots of outdoor play, there are two influential traditions shaping practice. The first is the elementary school tradition of Victorian England, where a hard surfaced and featureless school yard, used for short bursts of activity between lessons, characterised the outdoors. The adult supervisory role of this tradition predominates during playtimes in some schools to this day. However, educationally, the traditional playground is limited, providing few opportunities for children to manipulate, create, control or modify aspects of their environment. Additionally, it may present an intimidating barrier to social engagement for some children, particularly at transition points, such as starting full-time school. Therefore, the traditional playground represents the very antithesis of a responsive environment.

The second tradition of outdoor play draws on the contrasting image of a garden (Garrick, 2009). It has roots in the writings of Rousseau, an 18th-century philosopher, and his story of the fictional child Emile, exemplifying the educational value of children learning from firsthand experience in responsive environments. This tradition was enriched by European practice, particularly Froebel's early 19th-century kindergarten, and the McMillan sisters' open-air nursery school, developed in the slums of early 20th-century London. The McMillans' garden offered diverse experiences, with children free to play outside daily, for extended periods and through continuing changes in weather and seasons. It offered children rich opportunities to manipulate and create with natural materials, to build peer cultures and imaginative worlds. This tradition informs contemporary conceptualisations of the outdoors as a maximally responsive environment and a special place for play and learning. It is supported by three key areas of contemporary theory and research.

The first is the theory of learning dispositions underpinning Learning Stories, an innovative approach to assessment (Carr, 2001), and closely linked to Te Whāriki, New Zealand's early years curriculum framework (Ministry of Education, 1996). This narrative approach to assessment highlights early childhood as a critical period for strengthening five learning dispositions. Carr (2001: 24) highlights children's early interests in 'people, places and things', stimulated through their engagement in 'reciprocal and responsive relationships' (2001: 36). The case study material below exemplifies ways in which engagement with responsive outdoor environments can strengthen the dispositions of 'taking an interest', 'being involved', 'persisting with difficulty or uncertainty', 'communicating with others' and 'taking responsibility' (Carr, 2001: 24–5). This work underpins the rationale for responsive outdoor environments.

The second key area of contemporary theory and research is the new sociology of childhood, which foregrounds young children's interests in people. This theoretical perspective rejects traditional theories of socialisation, which position children as relatively passive subjects. It acknowledges children's agency within their social worlds. Corsaro (2005) presents examples of children actively creating peer cultures outdoors, from the self-organised ball, rope and skipping games of African American slave children before the Civil War, to the imaginative, outdoor play of three- and four-year-olds in a contemporary, Italian pre-school. His work offers fascinating insights into children's peer cultures and supports us in recognising their agency and related creativity. It prompts us to re-evaluate the extent to which our outdoor provision can support that agency and creativity.

The significance of responsive outdoor environments is underlined by a third key area of theory and research, focused on creativity. While Corsaro examines play from a sociological perspective, Anna Craft (2002) draws on psychological and philosophical perspectives to question traditional conceptualisations of creativity. She develops a theory of 'possibility thinking' (Craft, 2002: 91), which she sees as relevant in all areas of learning. Craft (2002: 113) proposes that adults support children to move beyond the initial question, 'What does this do?' to the more open-ended question, 'What can I do with this?' A conceptualisation of creativity as possibility thinking has real significance for our understanding of the potential and nature of responsive outdoor environments.

The potential for 'possibility thinking' outdoors is exemplified by Maxwell et al.'s (2008) study of the effects of introducing 'loose parts' or open-ended materials into an outdoor play area for four- and five-year-olds. Researchers provided new resources over a three-week period, including blocks, tyres, PVC pipes, fabrics and large branches. This encouraged children to explore the question, 'What can I do with this?' The study evidences how new materials, particularly larger blocks, supported children in 'place-making' (Maxwell et al., 2008: 40), described as the construction of defined, partly enclosed spaces that small groups of children then used as contexts for collaborative and dramatic play. The 'loose parts' created a highly dynamic, responsive environment, which extended the range of children's learning beyond the mainly physical learning first observed.

The section below provides further positive examples of children, from babies to primary school children, exercising agency outdoors, as they engage with people, places and things, and develop positive learning dispositions.

Principles into practice

These three key areas of theory and research provide a rationale for the principle of responsive environments. The implications for practice are examined below in relation to two contrasting case studies that offer starting points for practitioners seeking to answer the following interrelated questions:

- How can we design responsive outdoor environments that support the development of young children's creativity and dispositions for learning?

- What are the key elements to include in responsive outdoor environments that are dynamic, versatile and flexible in relation to spaces, resources, layout, planning and routines?

Working with babies, toddlers and young children (birth to 5 years)

Cherry Trees is a children's centre in a mixed community with pockets of social disadvantage. The manager and staff team have developed the garden over a period of two decades, working with a range of people and organisations. From a large, flat area of tarmac and grass, the team has developed four varied and attractive gardens. Planning supports children's decision-making and practitioners enhance the environment in relation to the changing interests of individuals and groups over the year. Routines are developed to ensure that all groups of children have the opportunity for extended periods of outdoor play on a daily basis.

Working with young children (5 to 7 years)

Greenlands is a rural infant school in an area of significant social disadvantage. Staff developed the garden with support from two lead artists from Creative Partnerships and local families. The garden project aimed to raise attainment in English, maths and science, through development of a broad and rich curriculum to excite and engage children. A further aim was to increase staff confidence to develop the curriculum in imaginative ways. The outcome is a varied and stimulating garden, used to support the formal curriculum for children from five to seven years and free play during school play-times. Nursery children also use the area, making this is a familiar place for children joining the main school.

The use of space and resources in the two gardens is examined below. Examples focus on the dynamic, versatile and flexible aspects of outdoor provision and the ways that outdoor play strengthens positive dispositions (Carr, 2001) and supports children's creativity or 'possibility thinking' (Craft, 2002).

Spaces

The children's centre and school gardens are designed to meet the principle of flexibility and versatility. Spaces are flexible, providing some defined and partly enclosed spaces that support social interaction but can be used in multiple ways. For example, the Cherry Trees gardens for babies and toddlers include the following enclosed and/or defined spaces:

- an empty wooden house with benches, a roof and windows

- a toadstool table and stools

- a willow tunnel

- a willow wigwam

- soft matting under a cloth sail attached to poles

- a pergola, partly covered in plants

- a small clearing amongst the trees.

The garden for three- and four-year-olds includes similar spaces but has more opportunities for children to create new spaces or extend existing spaces, using a range of resources.

Greenlands also provides flexible, partly enclosed spaces, designed in scale to meet the needs of older children. These include:

- a small, tangled area of shrubs and trees with a path running through, a small central clearing, and plastic piping for experimental sound-making

- a large wigwam structure

- a small performance area with a paved, circular stage and tiered seating.

Another design feature is the permeable or suggestive nature of some boundaries which define the space, but remain flexible for children wanting to join or leave the play. Across the two settings, permeable or suggestive boundaries include:

- upturned tyres

- a line of interlocking plastic tunnels

- tall grasses

- a line of small trees and bushes

- large rocks defining different levels of the garden

- contrasting ground surfaces, such as grass, decking, different kinds of paving, tarmac and bark chippings.

Varied pathways are another important design feature, supporting children in journeying from place to place. Journeying begins in very young children with the physical or sensory exploration of a path. It leads into journeys as a feature of narratives that link to 'place-making' (Maxwell et al., 2008: 40). Pathways in the two settings include:

- a bark-chip pathway that weaves through an area of wildlife plantings

- a paving-stone pathway around the vegetable garden

- a stepping-stone pathway through the willow tunnel and leading back towards the entrance

- a trodden grass pathway through the bushes, leading to the house

- a paved and winding pathway leading up the hill, linking structures and resource areas.

Resources

Children's learning begins with their interests in 'people, places and things' (Carr, 2001: 24), often in combination. At both settings, the principle of flexibility informs decisions about things or resources, as well as space.

Natural areas, plants and natural materials provide open-ended resources that vary with the seasons, supporting children's creative play and explorations. These include:

- leaves, seeds, berries, twigs and branches from native trees and bushes

- leaves, seeds, flowers, petals and seed heads from flowers and vegetables

- small animals found in cultivated and uncultivated areas, such as snails, worms, beetles, caterpillars, butterflies

- sand, soil, bark and water, alongside containers, tools and other resources for containing, emptying and moving these.

Both settings also provide for large-scale, improvised music-making, using reclaimed materials:

- a line of metallic trays, containers and pans strung along a fence, with beaters (Cherry Trees);

- a large structure of plastic barrels and piping, with beaters (Greenlands).

At Cherry Trees other resources, varying in scale and quantity according to age, support place-making. These include:

- blocks, planks, tyres, crates, PVC pipes, fabrics, large branches, water in various containers.

Mark-making resources further promote children's agency, providing opportunities for design and embellishment and support for dramatic play themes. These include:

- large chalks, water with brushes, mark-making sets in containers.

Finally, a relatively small number of favourite resources support children's journeying and dramatic play, including:

- dressing up clothes, bags and rucksacks, a toy dog, carts and trolleys, bikes, a tea set.

The outdoor stories below exemplify ways that young children creatively take ownership of responsive and open-ended spaces and resources.

 Case study – Toddlers' outdoor story (1–2 years)

Gina, Hakeem, Ben and Olly are interested in the wooden house as a special place to explore alongside their friends. As soon as the nursery door opens in the morning, they make their way along the trodden grass pathway to the house, and spend an extended period of time moving in, out and around the house; sitting on and clambering up the step; crawling or walking from side to side inside the house; climbing up and down on the benches; banging feet on the benches; batting the mobiles that hang from the overhanging roof; and peeping through windows. The children show a keen awareness of peers, implicitly recognising their shared ownership of the space despite the number of children playing together. They explore making friends, sometimes watching each other or smiling, and showing each other treasures, for example a 'mummy snail' from the garden. Some children initiate games of peek-a-boo with Jeannie, the adult observing from outside.

Image 5.1   A special place to explore

Case study – Young children's outdoor story (3–5 years)

Hera, Sophie and Tilly set out together down the pathway, through the small woodland, to the clearing. On the way they stop several times, filling the helmet cooking pot with grasses, bark, fallen leaves and seeds. The girls work excitedly together, sprinkling the ingredients into their special cake: 'We're going to cook it…This is the sugar…Do you want to help me put some sugar in here?'

Soon they are joined by Jabir, curious to see what is going on. Initially Jabir is rebuffed by Sophie, leading the play, 'it's only for girls, this cake.' Jabir, however, is not so easily dismissed and persists in his attempt to join the group, 'Well, I'm pretending to be a girl.' His persistence is rewarded, the girls accept this argument, and he joins the play.

The four children together enact the unfolding story, 'We need to pour out all the cake because the animals need to eat it'. Sophie tips cake from the pot and the children run away, back down the path, 'There's a tiger, there's a tiger…Pretend to be frightened!'

 Image 5.2   Collecting for cooking

Case study – Outdoor story for children in the early school years (5–7 years)

It is lunch-time and a sunny day. After lunch, a large group of Year 2 children run into the story garden. They pass the story-board sails, the story tree, and the children on stage, acting out nursery rhymes and practising their dancing show for the lunch-time supervisor. They proceed to the giant, blue and yellow sound-making structure, collect beaters from the half buried barrels, and move into position for the band to begin. Soon there is a group of six children, dancing and making improvised music. Tammy and Jamie explore sounds made by blowing through the different lengths of piping, while Aarti, Jeni, Josh and Mikael take on a drummer role, working together to beat out a pattern of fast, repetitive rhythms. Miss Jones briefly passes by, stopping to admire the music, but the children were performing for themselves and barely noticed the acclaim. Lunch-time ends and the children return their beaters, with some moving on to help younger children tidy their resources.

The Cherry Trees and Greenlands gardens all offer children dynamic spaces with opportunities for journeying, place-making, dramatic story-telling, music-making and scientific explorations. These gardens enable children of different ages, in groups of different sizes, to exercise agency. The gardens support 'possibility thinking' or creativity (Craft, 2002), as children approach the area thinking, 'What can I do with this space and/or these resources?' They also support the development of dispositions

Image 5.3   Making sounds with pipes and barrels

for learning (Carr, 2001), including 'taking an interest', which is strengthened as children shape places and things to meet individual and shared preoccupations. Additionally, children who experience a sense of ownership and control often begin to take responsibility for the well-being of friends. Children 'collectively construct friendships' (Corsaro, 2005: 144) and can often develop a sense of fairness and respect for each other's point of view through peer negotiation, particularly where they have opportunities to exercise agency in play.

Moving forward

Things to think about and do

Responsive adults

Reflection on the importance of responsive outdoor environments raises questions about the nature of the adult role in supporting young children's learning outdoors. There has been limited discussion of the adult role in this chapter despite recognition of the significance of adult–child interaction for children's learning in recent research. The outdoor stories have featured adults in walk-on

(Continued)

(Continued)

rather than leading roles. Jeannie, the adult in the toddlers' outdoor story, is an attentive observer who interacts only in response to children's invitation to play. Similarly, Miss Jones, in the school outdoor story, shows interest and appreciation of the children's music-making in passing. To support young children's agency and creativity outdoors, there are times when adults may need to observe from a discreet distance, intervening judiciously. This appears to contradict research findings about the importance of 'sustained shared thinking' (Siraj-Blatchford and Sylva, 2004). However, research highlights the potential for sustained shared thinking between pairs of children as well as between adult–child partners. Therefore, there may be times outdoors where the adult role is primarily to be responsive to young children's developing agency.

The two case studies represent settings where staff teams have invested significant amounts of time in reflecting on and making plans to develop responsive outdoor environments. The two decades of collaborative development at Cherry Trees highlights successful outdoor provision as a long-term project. However, there are some actions that can offer early success, whatever the starting point.

- Provide a new space, enclosed and/or clearly defined to support exploration and place-making, and then observe how the children use it. For example, make an improvised den with the children, perhaps using large pieces of fabric pegged to a fence, clothes horse or other structure.

- Add a small number of inexpensive and open-ended resources in response to these first observations. These could be resources to support journeying, for example bags and carts, and resources to support place-making, such as baskets of natural materials.

- Develop or extend a small area of natural planting; for example, allow a small area of grass to grow tall. Additionally, plant some sturdy and fast-growing plants with year-round interest and plants which are attractive to wildlife, such as teasels, sedum and sunflowers.

Longer-term actions need to build on the creative ideas of all key stakeholders: staff, children, parents and the wider community. It may be useful to involve external organisations with expertise in developing creative curricula and/or outdoor environments with strong natural features. Relevant organisations are Creative Partnerships, Learning through Landscapes and BTCV (British Trust for Conservation Volunteers).

Key messages

- Outdoor provision can, and should, offer young children an endlessly versatile, changeable and responsive environment for all types of play where they can manipulate, create, control and modify.

- Responsive outdoor environments can be characterised as dynamic, versatile and flexible.

- Responsive outdoor environments should contribute to the strengthening of children's learning dispositions, including taking an interest, being involved and taking responsibility. These dispositions provide a strong foundation for future development and learning.

- Responsive outdoor environments can support young children's agency within their social worlds and their developing peer cultures.

- We can best promote 'possibility thinking' and creativity by developing responsive outdoor environments that encourage children to raise the question, 'What can I do with this?'

- The space itself as well as resources, layout, planning, routines and adult interaction all need to be versatile, open-ended and flexible to maximise their value to the child.

Further reading and resources

Three areas of theory and research have informed the ideas in this chapter. Although the three key authors have not written specifically about outdoor play, their work can inform our thinking about the significance of responsive, outdoor environments for early development and learning.

Learning dispositions: Carr, M. (2001) *Assessment in Early Childhood Settings*. London: Paul Chapman.

Young children's agency: Corsaro, W.A. (2005) *The Sociology of Childhood* (2nd edn). London: Sage.

Creativity and 'possibility thinking': Craft, A. (2002) *Creativity and Early Years Education*. London and New York: Continuum.

Learning through Landscapes: http://www.ltl.org.uk

Offering rich experiences

Contexts for play, exploration and talk

Claire Warden

This chapter explores:

- **The right that young children have to a rich outdoor environment full of irresistible natural stimuli, contexts for play, exploration and talk**
- **A consideration of how we offer real experiences and contact with the natural world within a 'community'**

Value: Young children must have a rich outdoor environment full of irresistible stimuli, contexts for play, exploration and talk, plenty of real experiences and contact with the natural world and with the community.

The rationale for rich experiences outdoors

Through outdoor play, young children can learn the skills of social interaction and friendship, care for living things and their environment, be curious and fascinated, feel awe, wonder and joy and become 'lost in the experience'. They can satisfy their deep urge to explore, experiment and understand and become aware of their community and locality, thus developing a sense of connection to the physical, natural and human world.

A particular strength of outdoor provision is that it offers children many opportunities to experience the real world, to have first-hand experiences, do real tasks and do what adults do, including being involved in the care of the outdoor space. An aesthetic awareness of and emotional link to the non-constructed or controlled, multi-sensory and multi-dimensional natural world is a crucial component of human well-being, and increasingly absent in young children's lives. The richness of cultural diversity is an important part of our everyday world; this can and should be explored by children through outdoor experiences. Giving children a sense of belonging to something bigger than the immediate family or setting lays foundations for living as a community.

The term rich environment has been used very frequently and so it is perhaps worthwhile to consider what we mean by 'richness' in terms of outdoor environments. Is it a space that has everything? Or one that has nothing? Is it the complexity of resources or complexity of thinking? Is it the people in our lives? Is it our place within a community that gives us the tools to interpret and understand richness? Can it be bought or is it a gift when we feel it? Can we be 'taught' to see it when we have it? Is it subjective in its interpretation?

In life, we create spaces around ourselves that mean something to us and have a connection to us as individuals. Children move into spaces that we have created in the hope they will meet the motivation and connection they seek. The closer the match between the child and their experience at a root level, then the more likely that the learning will be assimilated for later recall. Yet we do not place enough emphasis on the voices of children to direct and influence the spaces that they exist within. What about the lost voice of a generation who have not had the experience of playing outside in nature: are they able to reflect on their 'richness' of experience? Can their children, in turn, re-connect them through their motivation and engagement?

Joseph Clinton Pearce (1977) uses the term *magical thinking* to describe the child's way of knowing the world. These primary perceptions, Pearce notes, 'are developmental in that they tend to disappear'. Such primary perceptions are referred to as 'bondings to the earth' (1977: 136), and Pearce suggests that interaction with the physical substance of the living earth (e.g., rocks, trees, wind) is critical to the child's developing brain and intelligence. Even in naturalistic spaces, these magical thoughts may not appear if the space is devoid of creative stimulus. In areas that are over-structured and directive, the opportunity to let go, to create and develop are limited. Where activity driven 'programmes' create a given context, they will reduce the motivation to talk and explore if the child perceives their engagement as being secondary to the experience.

In his seminal work, Csikszentmihalyi (1975) outlines his theory that people are most happy when they are in a state of *flow* – a state of concentration or complete absorption with the activity. Many writers have spoken of their connection to nature being in line with this. Wilson (1997) talks of her experience:

> ...picking cherries and plums from the trees in our yard, watching daffodils unfold in early spring, and rejoicing in the sweet scent of the lilacs that grew near our house. Such experiences filled my world with song, and I remember being swept away in a joyful childhood dance. Today, I miss the music, the dance, and the enchantment of childhood. 'Earth song' has been replaced by the noise of traffic, and daily life feels more like a race than a dance. The enchantment of knowing the world as a song is a treasured memory – a memory that still adds joy to my life. This memory, however, also brings a touch of sadness, because I feel that over the years to adulthood, I've truly lost something special along the way. This 'something special' is a way of knowing the natural world as a place of beauty and mystery. While I still maintain the belief that the world is full of mystery and wonder, my way of knowing it as such is not as direct and experiential.

The space created was enough to sweep her away in a joyful dance. The space, time and child came together to create a moment or a series of moments of connection. The context was one that was self-created as an interpretation and engagement with the natural environment around her. These memories have been retained by her into adulthood, and so tell us a great deal about the 'richness' of the moment.

Rachel Sebba (1991), a researcher from Israel, investigated children's relation to the environment from actual and retrospective points of view. In conducting her research, Sebba looked at the environmental preferences and the nature of the experiences of being outdoors as reflected in adults' recollections and in children's actual approaches to investigating the world. Her findings suggest that children experience the natural environment 'in a deep and direct manner, not as a background for events, but, rather, as a factor and stimulator' (1991: 395).

Sebba's findings are consistent with the work of Edith Cobb (1977), who concluded from her research that experience in childhood is never formal or abstract. 'Even the world of nature,' she says, 'is not a "scene," or even a landscape. Nature for the child is sheer sensory experience' (1977: 28–9). The context and its richness are supplied in a naturalistic outdoor space in a way that cannot be fully replicated by over-designed, closed materials for play.

Children seek contexts of excitement so that learning and discovery are at the very tip of the experience. When children decide to repeat an experience it is actually not static, it changes ever so slightly to assimilate new information, to make sure that each time the experience is different. Flemmen (2001) explores a concept of *systematic uncertainty* that children create in their play to make sure the outcome is unpredictable. It is this context of excitement that is a stimulus for play exploration. The talk wraps around the experience as a method of understanding, interpretation and sharing the moment with the community around the child.

The richness of a space can be linked to the level of *play affordance* proffered, or rather, what the loose materials within it offer. Many children seem to link more easily and directly with the open-ended materials that nature supplies. A stick must be the longest-standing toy of childhood. The concept of 'affordance' (Gibson, 1979) refers to what the environment offers; what it provides for the child. Affordances are opportunities that arise from the interaction between the physical properties of the environment and the interests, ideas and intent of the individual. Affordances arise through active detection: where the person is sensing and moving, observing and acting at the same time. This dynamic behaviour is the very aspect that attracts children to the outdoor environment. The richest contexts are linked to nature, so such things as mud and earth, winter holes, leaves, transparency, slope and gradients all repeatedly feature in our work in nature kindergartens. They reflect the motivation of children and the skill of the adults to create cross-references to the curriculum documents that seek to support work with children.

Any child will explore these open contexts. Schemas of repeatable divergent behaviours for the youngest children seem to be enabled to a greater degree than in convergent or structured spaces, but the concept of the schema, such as transporting, will be within the material interest of mud and earth. As the children mature, their schemas may move forward and combine, but the material context of the earth moves through an epistemic development to one of deeply understanding the material. This in turn leads to manipulation in order to sculpt and form. The context still has relevance to 5–7-year-olds as the creation of paint, ochre from the

Image 6.1   Deeply understanding the material

earth and application techniques all become about a more rigorous, detailed focus into the earth as a material.

In terms of children's play, the concept of affordance relates to what play possibilities are *afforded* by the physical environment. If the physical environment is over-designed and organised, it limits the very play it is trying to encourage.

Children play in response to both the objective and subjective qualities of an environment. Affordances are highly dynamic, with different features, elements and materials affording different play experiences for different individuals on different occasions. The number of affordances increases with the complexity of the environment. As highly complex environments, natural spaces provide limitless play affordances; the potential of the space matched by the inventiveness of the playing child. Through manipulating and changing more open-ended contexts and flexible environments through their play, children detect new affordances.

Principles into practice: what does this look like in practice?

Trees are a good example for us to explore across the age group of all the children in a setting. They have natural features that offer a large number of potential play affordances which in turn offer great provocations for talk.

Trees can be climbed and hidden behind; they can become forts or bases; with their surrounding vegetation and roots, they become dens and little houses; they provide

Image 6.2   Trees provide a backdrop for imagination

shelter, landmarks and privacy; fallen, they become part of an obstacle course or material for den-building; near them you find birds, little animals, conkers, fallen leaves, mud, fir cones and winged seeds; they provide a suitable backdrop for every conceivable game of the imagination (Ward, 1988).

Their place as a context is intertwined within their very play affordance. Let us take the experience of enclosure or den-building. A baby lying under the shade of the tree is in essence 'enclosed', stimulated by the light and movement. The tree as a place of context for experience offers many opportunities to be nurtured through nature. Den-building for a two-year-old is about thinking you are hidden when you cannot see the other person. For a four-year-old the den has become developed using the framing of the tree, the loose materials it offers to create features such as doorbells, window openings, bed areas and roof features such as chimneys. The complexity of thinking then moves into the use of tools and materials to develop and extend the concept of a den. Draft designs, a wider experience and knowledge of the types of dens and tree houses that could be built, use of tools and equipment such as saws, drills and measures, all deepen the learning and support children to create individual or small-group designs to keep the open-ended nature of the context.

The context of a tree also affords the learner an opportunity to talk about and consider the emotional aspects of their learning. Trees create shelter and privacy that are root experiences for all children, especially when the children are outside all year round. The seasonal variation offers more than printing with leaves. The youngest children feel the world through all their senses, so changing temperatures are good and should be experienced, through to the ground temperature and the

Image 6.3 Opportunity for being together

changing effects on leaves. Those settings running Forest School or who are moving towards a Nature Kindergarten will know that the context of a wood, a place of silence, has an emotive affect on the group; children and adults alike. In smaller spaces with a tree, or perhaps tree tubs, the context offers the opportunity to talk about how the presence of trees makes you feel, how we nurture and care for seedlings on a day-to-day basis, possibly leading to the design and building of supports, labels, information cards or 'This is my life' books.

Any natural environments containing many different species will extend the affordances of that space. For example, different trees drop their leaves at different times, produce different types of fruits and seeds, and their roots, trunks and branches grow in different ways. The bark and the very essence of trees are so very different. I am reminded of a little boy of three years old, who told me that every tree has a different song. What he had discovered was that his stick created a new sound according to the tree species, its size and age (growth rate). He had not yet acquired the language structure that would explain the different growth rates of species and the effect of climate or that the xylem and phloem inside the tree were acting as resonance tubes, but he did intuitively understand that they were all different because of what lay inside.

The tree features highly in terms of community: the marking of 'place' in public spaces; the meeting point in rural villages; the rite of passage for many adventurous children; the source of materials used for social play such as conkers and ash keys; the shade for picnics in the park. Trees are respected by many cultures and have

Image 6.4   Music on the tree

interdependence with the people that live near them for social connection, but also for herbal remedies, fire wood and sometimes spiritual connection. In some western cultures this has been lost; however, it has been interesting to see children, families and settings and their community coming together with a joint connection to plant trees in outdoor areas, or to recover small areas of community woodland to offer children the opportunity to 'be' in the woods. Perhaps this is because adults do understand the need for a connection to open contexts and the right to play in nature.

Moving forwards

Things to think about and do

- How can adults create time and space for open-ended investigations about small contexts to support deep-level involvement?

- Discuss the idea of 'play affordance' and how this thinking can enrich your outdoor play provision.

- Create nature spaces with loose materials to act as provocations for creative thinking.

- Explore the consultative strategies you have to find out what purposeful contexts are really of interest to children.

- Create opportunities to record talk through using Flip Mino™ cameras or similar, so that children's voices and motivations are heard throughout the planning procedure.

- Create a landscape area that is naturalistic, reducing the man-made plastic resources inside and outside for the younger children.

Key messages

- Through outdoor play, young children can learn the skills of social inter-action and friendship, care for living things and their environment, be curious and fascinated, feel awe, wonder and joy and become 'lost in the experience'.

- Children relating to the outside environment can satisfy their deep urge to explore, experiment and understand and become aware of their community and locality, thus developing a sense of connection to the physical, natural and human world.

Further reading and resources

Chawla, L. (2002) 'Spots of time: manifold ways of being in nature in childhood', in P. Kahn and S. Kellert (eds), *Children and Nature*. Cambridge, MA: MIT Press.

Warden, C. (2010) *Nature Kindergartens*. Auchterarder: Mindstretchers.

Warden, C. (2010) *Journeys into Nature*. Auchterarder: Mindstretchers.

7

As long as they need

The vital role of time

Di Chilvers

> **This chapter explores:**
>
> - **The need of children to spend extended periods outside**
> - **The freedom children need to take their time when playing outdoors**
> - **The benefits of slow learning**
>
> *Value: Young children should have long periods of time outside. They need to know that they can be outside everyday, when they want to, and that they can develop their ideas for play over time.*

As we get older time seems to fly by and we always end up rushing from one thing to another, with lives that are relentlessly busy, juggling jobs, homes and families. If we stop for a moment and think back to our own childhoods, no doubt our memories of playing with friends, paddling in the sea and creating secret dens will be punctuated with the memory of long days and time to soak ourselves in exciting games and activities. As a child I remember being able to play in our garden in the 'wendy house' mum had made out of old curtains, and the wooden slide down the garden steps made out of an old door. We had dressing-up clothes and used to spend hours together in imaginative play. Time was as long as it took, and we only came in for food and when it got dark.

Children have a unique ability to 'slow down' time. They don't want to be rushed from one thing to another, they want to 'wallow' in what they are doing; yet we impose on them an adult obsession with time. Mary Jane Drummond has written about children's education being like a 'rush up the motorway' with the adults keeping them on track and on target:

> What use is it to us, to have only a motoring map with a big fat blue line, impelling us to speed up it, never knowing, actually, where we are or where we might go? And what use are we then to the children we presume to educate! Driving headlong down the goals orientated motorway, we miss the wealth of possibilities to either side. (Drummond 1999, in Abbott and Nutbrown, 2001: 94)

Image 7.1   Hanging the washing

There is another view of time which sits much better with young children's development, but is equally relevant to us all:

> Allowing the mind time to meander is not a luxury that can safely be cut back as life or work gets more demanding. On the contrary, thinking slowly is a vital part of the cognitive armamentarium. We need tortoise mind just as much as we need the hare brain. (Claxton, 1998: 2)

Young children need time to meander and think slowly, a perspective which relates more to a sunny day on a winding country road rather than a motorway rush, with plenty of opportunities for 'picnics' where they can share rich experiences based on their interests and with adults who observe what they do and support what they need. It is these 'picnics' (experiences) which have deeper meaning for children and which will have a profound effect on them as thinkers and learners.

This chapter will look in detail at the reasons why *time* and opportunities for 'picnics' are such a crucial constituent of children's lives and learning, and why the adults who live and work with children should respect, value and uphold time outdoors. The underpinning principles and theory of 'time' for outdoor play will be considered, as well as how to establish good practice with all children, including babies and toddlers.

Why does time matter in outdoor play?

A recent visit to a children's centre in the north of England to observe outdoor play was a salutary lesson as to why children should have access to the outside for prolonged periods of time.

Case study – Playing with water

It was a chilly, windy day with intermittent drops of rain but the children were dressed for the weather with wellingtons, wet weather trousers and coats. The practitioners had organised a den with a large tarpaulin that kept blowing frantically in the wind, an easel for painting, musical instruments, a snack area, chalking on the blackboard on the side of the outside store, a dough table and some bikes in a separate area. There was a lot of choice and most of the adults were engaged with the children and leading the play.

The first 40 minutes outside was dominated by the well-meaning practitioners who had very close and positive relationships with the children. The children were happy to follow their suggestions and made the den bigger with tunnels at either end, although they had been fascinated by the way the wind was making it balloon out and two of the boys wanted to be monsters. The conversations were mainly led by the adults who asked the children if they wanted their snack or commented on the rain and the wind. Then the play began to change and the children took control and led the way for the next 40 minutes.

Dillon (just 3 years old) had been flitting from one activity to another when he suddenly found a green bucket (with no handle) and began to fetch water. He became completely focussed on transporting the water backwards and forwards; he did this 16 times, each time taking great care not to spill the water. He tipped the water in the plant trough to make mud and went to get some more, laughing to himself and walking very carefully to avoid other children. At one point a younger child took the bucket off him; fortunately a practitioner came to help and gave the younger child his own container. Dillon was the catalyst for the transporting play and others began to join in, including Kyle, who was older. Kyle's water transporting was at speed with water going everywhere, but the practitioners observed and at appropriate times suggested that he might not lose all the water if he went slowly. He tried this but preferred his own method; he wanted the water to splash.

As the play progressed, the children looked for any container, including the recently used cooking bowls, and the adults supported them as they struggled to turn on taps, fill and pour, balance and negotiate their way to the plant troughs.

During the last 40 minutes of outdoor play the children had become engrossed in their water play, with Dillon and Kyle deeply involved, concentrating and engaged in what they were doing. If the opportunity for outdoor play had been limited by time this would never have happened. Time for Dillon, Kyle and the other children was as long as it took.

So what can we learn from this observation about the importance of time outdoors?

In her extensive work on play, Tina Bruce (1991) talks about children being given the opportunity to 'wallow' in order to develop their 'ideas, feelings and relationships in an organic and unpressed way' (1991: 2), which is just what Dillon and Kyle were doing. Through this time to 'wallow', children become absorbed and involved at much deeper levels, and thinking moves from being superficial to deeply thoughtful and reflective. It is through this deeper thinking (often described as meta-cognition) that children begin to make connections in their learning and understanding. If Dillon and Kyle's time for outdoor play had been cut short, they would never have reached this deeper level of thinking.

Time for children to 'wallow', wonder and be curious form part of Bruce's (1991) theory of *free-flow play*, which is a term often used by settings to describe the practice of indoor and outdoor play being available at the same time. However, *free-flow play* is much more than this. Bruce describes 12 features of *free-flow play*, of which one is 'wallowing'; others include it being an active process which is intrinsically motivated by the child, and the need for first hand experiences (1991: 59). Opportunities for *free-flow play* can be initiated by children, either by themselves or in larger groups, and will be sustained for long periods, moving from the known to the unknown in the same way as Vygotsky's 'zone of proximal development' and sustained shared thinking. It is the *time* to initiate play, ask questions, problem solve, reason and reflect that children need in abundance, much more than they need expensive or elaborate equipment.

Guy Claxton describes 'slow ways of knowing' (1998: 4) where ideas and thinking emerge from uncertainty; and time to ponder, wonder and contemplate are essential spaces (picnics) for children (and adults) to seek out meaning and understanding. Outdoor play provides these crucial opportunities for 'slow thinking' and 'meandering' which children need much more of, particularly when more formal education begins. It is false economy to assume that children will do more thinking and learning whilst they are inside, usually at a table, with the 'deal' being that you can go out to play when you have finished your work! If children, especially boys, are given the time and space to do their thinking outside, the chances for them to become engrossed, involved and engaged will reap untold benefits as they learn in the state of 'relaxed cognition' (Claxton, 1998: 9) which frequently leads to sustained shared thinking and deeper levels of learning. This was evident in the 'transporting' play that Dillon and Kyle initiated and sustained.

Young children need time to experience and understand what they see, hear, feel, smell and taste. If we do a simple calculation, a two-year-old has actually only been in their world for 24 months or 730 days; it is not a long time, yet they are capable of so much. However, there is a propensity to 'hurry' children along: can they crawl, can they walk, can they run, hop, skip? Small children must have stretched arms as they hold onto a hand which is so high, and struggle along to keep up with the adult who is in such a hurry. A rushed and hurried pace becomes overwhelming and bewildering, even frightening and upsetting – children have their own pace:

> ...children have their own pace and while, as adults, we pursue our own (and others') timescales and agendas we need to be mindful of the need young children have to take their time. Pausing to listen to an aeroplane in the sky, stooping to watch a ladybird on a plant, sitting on a rock to watch the waves crash over the quayside – children have their own agendas and time scales, as they find out more about their world and make their place in it: they work hard not to let adults hurry them and we need to heed their message. (Nutbrown, 1996: 53)

For young children, the 'slow rhythms' (Cousins, 1999) and time to 'catch their breath' (Malaguzzi, quoted in Edwards et al., 1998: 80) that they need in their lives and learning, are an intrinsic part of being outside, where they become more relaxed and confident. It's easy to see, if we look properly, how children's synergy with the outdoors enables them to follow their ideas and interests in a different way

Image 7.2   Time for big ideas to emerge

to being inside. They should have the space for slow thinking, wallowing and exploring, without adult-imposed restrictions of time or inflexible routines. It is these opportunities which enable children to think creatively, build on their ideas with adult support, consolidate their new skills and repeat them in different ways. Susan Isaacs, writing in 1930, identified this time for children to think and catch their breath as the 'third generosity', where there was, 'an abundance of time for... thinking and doing. As a result the children were extraordinarily active, more active, more curious, more creative, more exploratory, more inventive than children in a less generous environment could ever be' (Rich et al., 2008: 34).

The other two generosities were related to the 'generous environment both indoors and outdoors in the large garden' and the children's 'big ideas' or interests, which Isaacs observed with a passion.

The adults' control over time can either support children's development, thinking and learning, or it can limit and squash it. Children, including toddlers, react in predictable ways when their time is restricted. They will quickly learn not to start anything, knowing that the adult will command them to stop in order to do some other task which is 'more important' than the child's. This 'stop/start' routine will inhibit children's engagement, concentration and involvement, the very dispositions we want to foster, and lead to a 'flitting' way of thinking. Then we wonder why children can't concentrate or focus on an activity!

The Early Years Foundation Stage (EYSF) guidance for England refers to 'schedules and routines which flow with the children's needs' and 'fit with children's rhythms'

(DCSF, 2008b), which a command to stop every 20/30 minutes for snack, group time, outdoor play or hall time definitely does not encourage. Adults can support and inspire children's thinking by playing with or alongside them, both indoors and outdoors, and as they build the learning together the adult can bring in the 'teaching' points to extend children's understanding. By tuning into the children's interests and taking the time to observe what they are doing, the adult will be weaving together the child's existing thinking and the new learning they may be ready to make. The crucial benefits here are that children, like Dillon and Kyle, are able to concentrate for long periods, develop their ideas and become involved in their thinking at a much deeper level, experiencing a concept known as 'flow' (Csikszentmihalyi, in Carr, 2001) that is central to children's learning. The conclusion is that children should not be stopped frequently, with their experiences and activities chopped into small chunks; the adults can move with them and through their observations decide when to intervene and offer support.

Another common reaction children have when time is restricted is the 'mad dash' (Lindon, 2001) or the 'hit and run' approach (Bilton, 2002) where children press their noses at the door eagerly watching you get the bikes out (why is it always bikes?) and then burst out in a frantic rush to grab what time they can outside before it is whisked away again. This unpredictable and inconsistent arrangement for outdoor play is counterproductive for everyone. For the children, their affinity and primary need to be outside is ruled by the weather (it's too cold, hot, wet, windy, foggy, snowy) and the adults who want to stay warm and dry! The clear message, that children quickly learn, is that time spent outside is to 'let off steam' or an opportunity for the adults to have a 'break'. The outdoors then becomes marginalised, with time indoors being seen as more important, and as a result we close down the rich potential for children's learning, most especially perhaps for the boys.

It is also important to consider the effect of this time-restricted approach on children's well-being and the anxiety that is brought about by a haphazard 'stop–start' regime, not knowing if they can go outside or being enclosed for long periods in a small room with limited space to move. Kyle and Dillon needed the space and time that being outside offered them and this doesn't change as children get older. Indeed they need more time outside when they can be physically active, using larger movements, refining hand–eye coordination and learning to control their bodies – significant skills for boys, particularly when they have to spend long periods of time in small cramped classrooms. In fact, we need to consider how much the restriction of time outside (the cause) is related to children's negative behaviour inside (the effect) and the impact this is having on well-being, self-esteem and learning. Children's challenging behaviour may be due to the time restrictions of the environment both inside and outside.

If outdoor play is available all the time, as part of continuous provision, children will be calmer and more relaxed, and there will be no need to abandon their activities inside because they can move outside whenever they need to, with the opportunity of being able to develop their play in both areas. The 'patrolling' outdoor role of the adult can disappear as children's play will not be a frantic rush and battle to claim their stake on the best bike or the climbing frame. Calmer outdoor environments are safer ones where children can freely wallow in their play with happy adults supporting them. A word of caution though, if you are moving from

Image 7.3   Time to persist and succeed

a rigid structured routine to a more flexible time outside there will be a period of disequilibrium which will need its own time to settle down.

What will this look like in practice?

For the adults/practitioners

People who are around children need to take the time to *listen* in a respectful and interested way which does not hurry or undervalue the child. Listening is about acknowledging and celebrating who we are, what we think and say and is also an act of affirmation and self-belief. Taking the time to do this is critical for everyone, especially for babies, toddlers and young children, because through this children will become confident, happy and inspired. Being outside is an ideal forum for listening through careful observations that document children's ideas and thinking as well as how they develop over time.

For babies, we can listen to their facial expressions and reactions to stimulus outside like wind and snow; for toddlers it may be listening to their actions and attempts at moving independently and their puzzled expressions as they come into contact with new materials and experiences. For very young children this takes time; time to absorb, understand and mesh new experiences with previous ones.

We also need to give children time to vocalise their ideas, thinking and feelings. Adults asking too many questions, hurrying them to answer and giving little time to think and compose their thoughts is a common problem which renders children silent and disempowered. Children need thinking time: 'Whatever form of communication is used, children need space and time to respond and to know that the practitioner is giving full attention and encouragement to their thinking' (DCSF, 2008b: 2.3 Supporting Learning).

Adults also need time; time to do their own thinking, to understand why children do what they do and to make sense of their observations. Through taking time to do this, adults will build their knowledge, experience and confidence and ensure good practice is embedded.

For the children

The EYFS guidance asserts that children need plenty of space and time to play, both outdoors and indoors (DCSF, 2008b: 4.1 Play & Exploration). Babies, toddlers and young children need to have the time and opportunity to repeat their actions and ideas as well as to return to 'projects' to continue their work, refine their thinking and process what they have learned. For babies this may be around experiences with natural materials outside, like sand and water or experiencing the feel of grass and the smell of flowers. For toddlers, time outside will support their growing independence and movement with opportunities to explore their interests and practise new skills. Dillon is a good example of how his interest in transporting water gave him the time to 'concentrate on activities and experiences to develop their own interests' (DCSF, 2008b: 4.4 Learning & Development). Older children need time to build their ideas, try things out, make mistakes and try again in the security of an environment that doesn't rush them. The EYFS acknowledges that this can be a 'long process' (DCSF, 2008b: 4.3 Creativity & Critical Thinking) which adults need to recognise and provide for.

When children are outside they tend to talk more readily and engage in conversations with each other and with adults. Time to talk is crucial as this is one of the main ways in which children communicate their thinking, ideas and feelings. There is an inherent freedom of the outdoors which allows children to follow their interests, ideas and conversations and which adults need to capture and build on. This is particularly important for children learning English as an additional language, where time to absorb, adjust and practise language is the main resource they need to support their learning and development (Chilvers, 2006).

For the environment

The rich resources we need for an enabling early years environment are time, well-qualified adults, open-ended materials and the consistent use of the outdoors for babies, toddlers and young children. There is a misguided belief that provision for the outdoors is expensive (why do we buy so many bikes?), requires vast spaces (it is what you do with the space that counts) and architectural landscaping! Children rather need creative adults who will provide open-ended materials (none better than the cardboard box) based on their accumulated observations of children's development, needs and interests over time. Guidance frameworks for early childhood education in all the countries of the UK reinforce this, and in doing so give settings underpinning principles for good practice.

Moving forwards

 Things to think about and do

As a team, reflect upon and evaluate how children experience time in your outdoor provision. For example, do all children have:

- time to wallow in order to develop their 'ideas, feelings and relationships in an organic and unpressured way'?
- time that enables them to become absorbed, involved and engaged, developing their thinking and concentration?
- time to listen and time to talk?
- time for consistent outdoor play which gives them the inherent freedom to follow their interests, ideas and conversations?
- time to initiate play, ask questions, problem solve, reason and reflect?
- time to ponder, wonder and contemplate providing essential spaces (picnics) for children (and adults) to seek out meaning and understanding?
- time to think creatively, build on their ideas with adult support, consolidate their new skills and repeat them in different ways?
- time that is flexible and fits with their own rhythms?
- an absence of time restrictions in the indoor and outdoor environment that have a negative impact on their behaviour?
- time outside which is continuous, leading to a calmer outdoor environment where they can feely wallow in their play with unhurried adults supporting them?
- time to talk so that they can communicate their thinking, ideas and feelings?

Key messages

- High quality play outdoors, where children are deeply involved, only emerges when they know they are not hurried.
- Children need to have time to develop their use of spaces and resources and uninterrupted time to develop their play ideas, or to construct a place and then play in it or to get into problem-solving on a big scale.
- They need to be able to return to projects again and again until 'finished' with them.
- Slow learning is good learning, giving time for assimilation.

- When children can move between indoors and outside, their play or explorations develop further still.

- Young children also need time (and places) to daydream, look on or simply relax outside.

Further reading and resources

Bruce, T. (1991) *Time to Play in Early Childhood Education.* London: Hodder and Stoughton.

Claxton, G. (1998) *Hare Brain, Tortoise Mind: Why Intelligence Increases When You Think Less.* London: Fourth Estate.

Gussin Paley, V. (2004) *A Child's Work: The Importance of Fantasy Play.* London: The University of Chicago Press.

Achieving the balance

Challenge, risk and safety

Helen Tovey

This chapter explores

- **Evidence of the value of risk and challenge in play outdoors**
- **Implications for practice**
- **Critical reflection on attitudes to risk-taking and adventurous play outdoors**

Value: Young children need challenge and risk within a framework of security and safety. The outdoor environment lends itself to offering challenge, helping children to learn how to be safe and to be aware of others.

Watch young children playing outdoors and they seem drawn to activities such as climbing high, sliding fast, swinging, rolling, balancing and hanging upside down. Outdoors offers rich potential for such challenging play as it provides the space, freedom and opportunity to explore limits. Yet research (Tovey, 2010) suggests that while some practitioners support and encourage such adventurous play outdoors, many feel anxious and reluctant to allow children to take any risks for fear of accident and blame.

Risk has become something to be regulated, assessed, managed, controlled and in many cases removed. Practitioners on in-service courses have reported that equipment such as slides or climbing frames have been removed, trees cut down, children stopped from sliding headfirst down a slide, or playing out of sight in bushes amid a climate of risk aversion. Yet the problem with this approach is that it assumes that by removing risk, children will be safer as a result. It fails to acknowledge risk as a positive feature of children's learning and is rarely balanced against the play value of the experience itself. Other discourses emphasise more positive features of risk. The Royal Society of Arts Commission on Risk and Childhood defines risk as 'perceptions of dangers and uncertainties that may have negative outcomes but which may also be undertaken with positive consequences' (Madge and Barker, 2007: 10). Similarly, Little (2006) emphasises the element of uncertainty and argues that risk-taking requires a consideration of the benefits against the possible undesirable consequences of the behaviour as well as the probability of success or failure. So what are the benefits of risk-taking in play outdoors?

Firstly, risk is part of being alive and being human. Babies would never learn to crawl, negotiate steps, stand up, or children learn to run, ride a bike and so on without being prepared to take a risk, to tumble and to learn from the consequences. Learning to navigate space, people and objects requires risk and a willingness to try things, have a go and make mistakes. As Moss and Petrie argue 'risk is inherent in human endeavour, and for children not to engage with it is for them to be cut off from an important part of life' (2002: 130).

The willingness to take risks is also an important learning disposition. Research by Dweck (2000) emphasises the importance of what she terms a 'mastery' approach to learning – a disposition to have a go, try something out and relish challenge, in contrast to a 'helpless' approach characterised by fearfulness and fear of failure. When we repeatedly say to children 'mind out'; 'be careful'; 'don't do that'; 'come down you'll fall', there is a danger that we help shape this 'helpless' attitude to learning by communicating our own anxiety. To have a good disposition to learn requires confidence, competence and willingness to have a go. Play outdoors motivates children to extend their own boundaries, to be adventurous, to explore a little further and to engage with risk in a controlled and supportive environment. Environments where children are discouraged from taking risk, where adults themselves are anxious and fearful, are less likely to develop the disposition to persist, to see challenges as problems to enjoy rather than things to fear. As Dweck argued, 'it doesn't help a child to tackle a difficult task if they succeed constantly on an easy one. It doesn't teach them to persist in the face of obstacles, if obstacles are always eliminated' (Dweck, cited in Claxton, 1999: 35).

Risk-taking in play appears to be positively associated with emotional well-being, resilience and mental health. A report by the UK Mental Health Foundation argued that free play outdoors, 'enables children to take risks, to think through decisions and gain increased self-confidence and greater resilience' (Mental Health Foundation, 1999: 36). The report argued that the lack of opportunity to experience risk in play outdoors was damaging children's well-being and resilience. It appears that rather than protecting children from risk, controlled exposure to some risks can itself be protective. Kloep and Hendry (2007) draw on Rutter's notion of 'steeling experiences' to argue that mistakes, providing they are not overly disastrous, can offer protection against the negative effects of future failure. Managing fear and uncertainty and holding your nerve when feeling on the edge of 'out of control' are important aspects of emotional well-being.

Spinka, Newberry and Bekoff (2001) suggest that adventurous play is characteristic of play in all mammals and serves as 'training for the unexpected'. They argue that players deliberately put themselves in disadvantageous positions and that novelty and risk add to the intensity and pleasure of the play. Players switch playfully between well-controlled movements and those where they experience being on the edge of out-of-control. Such play, they argue, increases the range and versatility of movement and helps players cope physically and emotionally with unexpected events.

Image 8.1   The exhilaration of a rope swing

Physical risk-taking in play often involves vigorous movements such as swinging, tipping, hanging and rolling, where normal balance and posture is distorted. Research by Greenland (2006) suggests that such movement play is vital in stimulating young children's vestibular and proprioceptive senses; that is, their sense of balance and sense of self in space. She argues that the absence of such physically challenging play can contribute to clumsiness, attention problems and later learning difficulties.

Evidence on the links between movement and cognition suggest that whole-body experiences of a varied terrain outdoors are highly important not only for developing physical skills but also for developing key mathematical and scientific concepts (Athey, 1990). Adventurous play outdoors can enrich and extend the range of experiences which support such conceptual development. For example, sliding headfirst down a slide offers experience of such things as direction, gradient, speed and concepts of headfirst or even headfirst backwards. Swinging on a rope can provide experience of such concepts as energy, forces, gravity, speed, distance, cause and effect. Yet such experiences are often denied to children in early years settings as being 'too risky'. Confining children to flat, rubberised safety surfaces, denies children the essential aspects of conceptual learning.

Lastly, there can be great joy and delight in play where risk itself is the main attraction and motivation to continue. The simultaneous feeling of risk and challenge, fear and exhilaration, control and lack of control can be considered a characteristic of such play, whether in babies' precarious delight at being thrown in the air, bounced vigorously or tipped backwards, in young children's joy in balancing along a wobbly bridge or in older children swinging on the end of a rope. Adults'

Image 8.2   Dizzy play

enjoyment of activities such as skiing, zip-wire riding or sledging can evoke similar exhilarating enjoyment. Caillois refers to such experiences as *ilynx* or 'dizzy play' (Kalliala, 2006). *Ilynx* is the Greek word for whirling water, and dizzy play often has this freewheeling, spinning, exhilarating quality. Caillois identifies the 'voluptuous panic' that such play can engender. He argues that such experiences are important elements of group camaraderie, friendship and social cohesion (Caillois, 2001).

Clearly risk-taking is not all positive. Children can learn to take risks which are inappropriate, which border on recklessness or which put themselves or others at risk of serious injury. As in many areas of learning, children need the guidance of experienced others who can help them recognise serious risk and teach safe ways of doing things, but who also encourage a positive disposition to adventure and challenge.

While few would disagree with the need to ensure young children's safety in their play outside, there is much less agreement as to what is meant by such phrases as 'keeping children safe'. Many early years settings have as part of their statement of aims a phrase such as, 'we aim to create a safe, secure and stimulating environment'. However, given the widespread evidence that children can actually be 'too safe for their own good' (Lindon, 2003), is absolute safety an appropriate aim and can it ever be achieved? Should we seek to make environments as safe as possible or should we, as the Royal Society of Prevention of Accidents (RoSPA) has suggested, make environments just as safe as necessary? There is an important distinction here. It could be argued that an environment which is as safe as possible, where all possible sources of risk of harm are removed, is actually an unsafe environment as it offers little play value and denies children the necessary experience to develop and practice the skills to be safe. Children in such environments may seek adventure and challenge in more reckless ways or alternatively they may learn to be compliant, unadventurous and risk averse and miss out on important learning experiences. As the UK Health and Safety Executive have stated, 'we must not lose sight of the important developmental role of play in pursuit of the unachievable goal of absolute safety' (cited in Ball et al., 2008: 117).

Clearly children learn from mistakes, accidents do happen and bumps, bruises, trips and tumbles are an important part of learning. Our responsibility is to ensure that risk of significant injury is minimised. This means knowing children well, trusting children to recognise their own limits, teaching children to do things safely and ensuring that they have opportunities to take part in experiences which feel satisfyingly scary but which do not expose them to inappropriate risk or hazards.

What are the implications for practice?

It is important to recognise that there is no such thing as 'risk' in reality. Risk can mean different things to different people. What is an acceptable risk to one child might be a hazard to another. What is commonplace in one culture is considered dangerous in another. It is therefore inappropriate to list experiences which children should or should not engage in at various ages. Where children have had regular experiences of challenging activities outdoors their competence and confidence will be much greater than when children have had little experience. Nevertheless, creating an environment which offers diverse opportunities for challenging play is essential.

Creating a challenging environment

A challenging environment needs to be flexible enough for individuals and groups of children to find and pursue their own challenges and will vary for different age groups. Nevertheless an environment for challenging, adventurous play is likely to include:

- Experience of nature with a wide range of trees, bushes and plants offering rich scope for play. For example, staff in a Children's Centre included teasels and thistles amongst the plants in their garden for under-threes. A group of toddlers spent a long time trying to fix a clothes peg on to the prickly stem of a teasel plant. They were both fascinated by and fearful of the prickles.

- Uneven ground that children can navigate, such as grassy banks for clambering and rolling, slopes for sliding, tunnels for crawling, ditches for crossing.

- Resources which allow opportunities for swinging, sliding, balancing, crawling and climbing, so that children can move their bodies in space. Resources must be flexible enough to ensure challenge for the most timid and the most adventurous. For example, a workplace nursery positioned an enclosed fabric and rope swing over a sand pit. The toddlers enjoyed pushing each other on the swing and the three-year-olds enjoyed twisting the rope resulting in rapidly rotating movements as the rope unwound. The sand provided a soft landing for any falls.

- Loose parts and open-ended materials such as cardboard boxes, crates, blankets, wheels, planks. Such props can increase the degree of challenge as they can be combined in a variety of ways, unlike fixed, static equipment.

- Opportunity to experience increasingly fast speeds, whether on rope swings, slopes for wheeled toys, slides which can be positioned at ever increasing gradients or slopes for sliding or rolling.

- Resources which give a sensation of instability such as rockers, 'swing' bridges, rope bridges, see-saws. These offer unpredictability and sense of risk without any danger.

- Ropes which can be attached to fixed rings to enable children to climb slopes, steep banks or to cross wide ditches.

- Features which allow children to experience height without risk of fall. For example a primary school in London created an aerial walkway through trees. The children could traverse the high ground safely but the height made the experience satisfyingly 'scary'.

- Flexible resources which can be combined in different ways providing increasing levels of challenge. For example, tubes, crates and lengths of guttering can offer exciting and challenging play with balls, water or sand for all children from about one year onwards. A primary school reception class developed an exciting project focusing on the flow of water. Hose pipes, guttering, tubes of plastic piping and a water wheel were used by the children to create elaborate constructions. Children used a mobile ladder to reach the top levels. Adults supported their problem solving but also taught them safe ways of using the ladder.

Despite the importance of a challenging environment, research by Stephenson (2003) emphasised children's hunger for physical challenge was satisfied more through the practitioners' attitudes than the provision itself. For example, adults who enjoyed being outside, who were interested in physical play and took a sensitive and liberal approach to supervision, enabled children to find challenges that were experienced as risky but which did not put them in a position of hazard. As Sandseter (2007, 2009) noted, when practitioners regard risky play as positive and necessary, they are willing to support children's reasonable risk-taking, even when this exceeds their own tolerance of risk. Tovey's (2010) research suggested that where practitioners felt supported within their teams and understood the benefits of risk-taking, they were confident to offer experiences which included some element of risk and challenge. Where practitioners felt unsupported by senior staff and anxious about blame and possible litigation they were less likely to make provision for adventurous play. Clearly, adults have key roles in supporting opportunities for challenging play. These include:

1 Developing shared understandings and expectations about the value of risk and the meaning of safety so that staff feel supported and 'safe' to be risk-takers themselves. This means engaging in debate and developing a shared approach to risk and safety which goes well beyond procedural risk assessments.

2 Engaging parents and the wider community in discussing issues around safety in play outdoors. This is essential if shared understandings are to be achieved and parents are to be seen as partners rather than critics or potential litigators. One school in London placed a huge poster in the entrance hall of the nursery proclaiming 'risky play is encouraged here' and showing examples of photos of adventurous play with captions explaining the processes of learning. This allowed issues to be discussed informally with parents. Staff told parents that

they could not guarantee that accidents would not happen but explained what they did to promote safety.

3 Having realistically high expectations of what children are able to do. This will involve knowing children well enough to make informed decisions as to when to intervene and when to stand back.

4 Learning from the Forest School movement where positive risk-taking is a central part of the philosophy. Children as young as three play in the woods, climb trees, slide down muddy banks, build dens and fires and use real tools such as saws and knives. Children are taught how to engage in such experiences safely; for example, how to whittle wood with the knife facing away from the body. One Children's Centre with regular access to a woodland environment taught children how to use a stick to test the depth of wet or muddy ground before stepping in it. This is a life skill which can help all children to be safe.

5 View children as risk-seekers and risk-takers with risk as an essential feature of children's play. This means tuning in to children's intentions and supporting them in finding safe ways of achieving what they want to do.

6 Developing a language with which to talk about risk and safety, for example, 'coming down backwards might be a safer way' or 'Josh found a very safe way of doing that – shall we see how he did it?' This also means being prepared to say a firm 'no that's dangerous because ….' in the rare situations it is needed. Children can feel safer to take risks and be adventurous when there are clear and reasonable boundaries.

These are just some examples. More detail about the principles underpinning a challenging environment can be found in Tovey (2007). Of crucial importance is

Image 8.3   Having high expectations

Image 8.4   The biggest risk is that there is no risk at all

that we open up a debate, with colleagues, parents and the wider community on the significance of risk-taking in childhood. If we deny children the opportunities to be risk-takers, we may paradoxically risk creating a generation of children who may be either reckless in their pursuits of thrills and excitement or risk-averse, lacking the confidence and skill to be safe but also lacking the disposition to be adventurous, creative and innovative in their thinking. As Bundy et al. (2009) argue, the biggest risk is that there is no risk at all.

Moving forwards

 Things to think about and do

- Are there opportunities in your setting for children to be adventurous in their play? Are there regular opportunities for play which they find enjoyably scary?

- Reflect on gender differences in attitudes to risk. Is risk tolerated or encouraged more in boys' than in girls' play? Little (2006) cites research which suggests that it is.

- What do you mean by the phrase 'keeping children safe'? Is it as safe as possible or just as safe as necessary? Think about the restrictions you impose. Are they always necessary?

- To what extent can you empower children to keep themselves safe? How can you support them in this?

(Continued)

(Continued)

- How can you make provision for children with disabilities to experience adventurous play; for example the exhilaration of moving at speed?

- Work together with colleagues to develop a shared approach to risk and safety outdoors. Discussing the document *Managing Risk in Play Provision: Implementation Guide* (see further reading) could be a useful starting point for reflection.

- Consider the environment you offer using the points above as a framework. How can you make more provision for adventurous and challenging play?

Key messages

- In-depth discussion with all stakeholders surrounding the significance of risk-taking and adventurous play in early childhood is crucially important.

- Children are seriously disadvantaged if they do not learn how to approach and manage physical and emotional risk. They can become either timid or reckless, or be unable to cope with consequences.

- Risk-taking allows children to develop confidence, positive attitudes, creativity and a sense of adventure.

- The outdoor environment lends itself to offering adventure, challenge and risk within a framework of security and safety, while helping children to learn how to keep themselves safe.

- Young children need to be able to set and meet their own challenges, become aware of their limits and push their abilities (at their own pace), be prepared to make mistakes, and experience the pleasure of feeling capable and competent. Challenge and its associated risk are vital for this. Young children also need to learn how to recognise and manage risk as a life-skill, so as to become able to act safely, for themselves and others.

- Safety of young children outdoors is paramount and a culture of 'benefit-risk assessment' or 'risk management to enable' that permeates every aspect of outdoor provision is vital for all settings.

Further reading and resources

Ball, D. Gill, T. and Spiegal, B. (2008) *Managing Risk in Play Provision: Implementation Guide*. London: Department for Children, Schools and Families.

Gill, T. (2007) *No Fear: Growing Up in a Risk Averse Society*. London: Calouste Gulbenkian Foundation.

Tovey, H. (2007) *Playing Outdoors: Spaces and Places, Risk and Challenge*. Maidenhead: Open University Press.

Outdoor play for everyone

Meeting the needs of individuals

Theresa Casey

This chapter explores:

- **How does, or could, outdoor provision support inclusion?**
- **What are the links between play and the right to be included?**
- **Which features and qualities are supportive of inclusive environments?**
- **How might we move towards more inclusive play environments?**

Value: Outdoor provision must support inclusion and meet the needs of individuals, offering a diverse range of play-based experiences.

Better play environments support inclusion; inclusive environments support play

Whether the motivation for improving an environment is inclusion or better play there are reciprocal benefits when improvements are made.

Play environments which are flexible, varied, challenging, intriguing and so on (all the qualities which reflect an understanding of play as chosen and controlled by the child) absorb very diverse and wide-ranging play behaviours. In environments without these qualities, we make it much harder for children to be able to play in the way they need to or would choose.

All children bring their own uniqueness into play – their experience, outlook, genetic history, personality, aspirations and perception of the world – and the way they choose to play will be driven by these and other variables. In early years settings it may be that the play of some children does not feel or look quite like the play of the majority. (For example it may seem more repetitive, draw on sensory experiences to a greater degree or appear more fleeting than that of other children.) Boys in particular may really benefit from space to make a lot of noise,

Image 9.1   Every child brings their own uniqueness into play

to involve themselves in rough and tumble play and very active forms of learning. The varied experience children bring with them of making use of natural resources will qualify the way and pace at which they use the resources the setting makes available. There are numerous other examples of how children's play will vary not simply by age or stage but through the complexity they themselves bring to play situations.

If the conclusion from that is, as I believe, that the wider the variety of play and ways of playing the environment supports, the more inclusive it is of children with a wide range of abilities and needs, then we should ask: what types of spaces are supportive of wide-ranging play and therefore inclusion?

We will return to this, later in the chapter.

Play rights and the right to be included

The term inclusion always bears some scrutiny and 'inclusive play' is used in numerous ways. There are those definitions that emphasise equal access and equal participation for example:

> Inclusive play is primarily about all children and young people having equal access to – and equal participation in – local play, childcare and leisure opportunities. (National Children's Bureau, 2006: 1)

Those that focus on the removal of disabling barriers, for example:

> Environmental barriers that exclude children with impairments ... can easily be changed and are not necessarily expensive. Social barriers such as fear, embarrassment or discriminatory attitudes also need to be tackled so that an accessible play space is also an inclusive one in which disabled children and their families feel welcome. The essential ingredient for making play space accessible is a willingness to seek out and remove disabling barriers. (Office of the Deputy Prime Minister, 2004: 3)

and the very play-focused definitions, such as:

> [Inclusive play means] enabling every child to play and express themselves in their own way and supporting children to play together when they wish to. (McIntyre, 2007: 5)

and

> From the very earliest age, disabled children should have the right to play and learn with other children, enjoying all the aspects of life and friendships that other children do. (Every Disabled Child Matters, *Inclusion Charter*)

It is of course in article 31 of the UN Convention on the Rights of the Child (UNCRC) that the right of every child to play is set out and, like all rights in the Convention, article 31 applies to every child; restricted opportunities for play have been described as a form of discrimination (United Nations Committee on the Rights of the Child, 2005: 5).

There is a strong link between the right to play and article 23 of the UNCRC, the right of disabled children to 'enjoy a full and decent life'.

> The attainment of full inclusion of children with disabilities in the society is realized when children are given the opportunity, places, and time to play with each other (children with disabilities and no disabilities). (United Nations Committee on the Rights of the Child, 2006: 19)

Arguments made elsewhere in this book give the case for the benefit of play outdoors, and of course it follows that all children are entitled to expect the same quality of experience and range of opportunities afforded their peers regardless of their background, race or disability, etc., a principle that we expect within all children's services (see 'Purpose and aims' of the Early Years Foundation Stage (DSCF, 2008b: 7) for example).

Features of an inclusive play environment

Beyond equality of opportunity, those in close contact with children at play outdoors often observe that for some children the very nature of outside space is particularly suitable: the sensory and aesthetic qualities, the opportunities for movement and expansiveness, the availability of space to make choices, the potential for contact with nature, can all be made available in greater abundance in the outdoors.

It is rarely if ever possible to make accurate predictions of specific features that will best suit particular children or groups of children, but there are a number of dimensions that are useful to consider above and beyond those you would expect to find in a 'good' play environment (flexibility, 'changeability', variety, natural features, a sense of place, etc.). These include:

- whether time has been taken to identify and remove or minimise disabling barriers

- the extent to which the environment supports children to play without the need for sophisticated language and play skills (see 'centres of interest' below)

- the extent to which children are able (permitted) to change and make use of features of the environment

- the availability of shelter and spaces with varied scale and properties

- the extent to which practitioners make time to observe play within the environment reflect on it and make adjustments to the environment on an ongoing basis

- the policy and attitude towards enabling risk, challenge and uncertainty in the outdoor environment.

Removing disabling barriers

It is generally accepted that it is not possible to make every single feature of a play space accessible in the same way for every child, nor would that be a sensible or achievable goal (Office of the Deputy Prime Minister, 2004: 3). However, all children should be supported to play in the way that they would choose and identification of barriers, or the conditions that cause them, is an important step. Barriers to play can be highly specific to an individual child so creating an inclusive environment should always be seen in context.

Here are just a few examples of steps that could be taken to change from a barrier-filled environment (environmental, social and organisational) to a more inclusive one.

Environmental:

- a single hard surface replaced by a variety of tarmac, grass, sand and grit surfaces

- standard swing seats replaced by widely available bucket, basket or hammock styles

- a monotonous aesthetic or monoculture environment broken up: by landmarks, sculptures and artworks; by changes in the quality of light; through planting for seasonality; by use of colour and contrast.

Social:

- discriminatory attitudes and practices tackled through equality training; disability awareness; social contact between families; development of policies and practices; action taken where discrimination persists.

Organisational:

- limited access to the outdoors replaced by continual access policies

- restrictive rules about how the outdoor environment is used examined and modified

- restrictive attitudes to the types of play that are accepted and encouraged, reflected on and modified.

Centres of interest

Observation of children at play reveals that from an early age children use very sophisticated communication skills – verbal and non-verbal communication, body language, facial expressions, eye contact, expressive noises. Formal and informal rules are developed both by children and adults which create additional layers of complexity. The poverty of many play environments – with monotonous grey tarmac, few natural features and the lack of loose materials – gives children few options but to join in play through communication and social skills. For children who are communicating differently, at a different level or with less well developed social competence than their peers, this can pose a real difficulty.

The principle of 'centres of interest' (developed in the Play Inclusive Action Research project) is to incorporate features that draw children to play around them in a way that allows them to be part of a realm of activity, interacting with others on a variety of levels – taking turns, laughing, chasing, copying, leading, following and so on – without necessarily having to engage in direct communication.

Centres of interest can be created in endless ways – swathes of beautiful fabric billowing in the wind; mud, sand and water play areas (see case study); a box of dressing up clothes; rough and ready dens and tents.

Change

To have an ever-evolving environment is on most practitioners' 'wish list', whether that is planting that changes with the seasons or major physical changes that take place through the way children play (such as digging and building). It reflects the aspiration to have a lively resource, responsive to children's changing needs.

An environment must work for the child rather than the child having to work to fit in with the environment (reflective of the social model of disability rather than the medical mode in this respect). For many children, making use of the resources an environment offers provides very immediate and important experiences of mastery and control. These might otherwise be in short supply if a child spends a great deal of time having medical treatment, caring for family members, or in erratic

Image 9.2   Centres of interest encourage interaction

family situations, for example. Ideas for providing a rich range of manipulable resources and loose materials are given in other chapters; see also Casey (2007) and White (2008).

Shelter and spaces with varied scale and properties

Sudden loud noises, high winds, too much bustle and other environmental occurrences can have adverse, sometimes hidden, impacts for particular children, such as causing sensory overload, confusion or distress. Lack of confidence and reluctance to join in can be the result of difficulty in navigating and making sense of the space. The features that might help to counteract this are also supportive measures to play generally. Creating divisions of space by using natural features such as slopes and shrubs, temporary features such as tepees or dens and the overlooked 'nooks and crannies' can break a whole environment down into more intimate, comfortable and manageable spaces. You could think of the outdoor provision as a series of informal 'rooms', generating their own identities as spaces.

Observation

The cycle of observation, reflection and adjustment of the environment in the light of observations is fundamental to sustaining an inclusive outdoor space. A useful way to check out observations from different angles is to hold team discussions at the end of play sessions, in which the perspectives of each member of the team are gathered. This has the benefit of providing an overview of the session, illuminating different interpretations and allowing a fuller picture to unfold. More experienced staff can pass on knowledge and skills and fresher ideas can be introduced. Teams might generate their own sets of 'prompts' to think about questions such as what the children gained from the session, the role of adults, how environmental features helped or hindered inclusive play. The team may choose to have a particular focus for a period of time (play types, risk and challenge, levels of intervention and so on) or create detailed pictures of the play of particular children, generating suggestions for extending, supporting or enhancing that child's personal and social experience.

Risk, challenge and uncertainty in an inclusive outdoor environment

Play advocates and theorists have long described the important qualities of play in terms of spontaneity, unpredictability and choice, and have recognised the need children have to challenge themselves and test their own limits. Children appear to generate 'uncertainty' in their play, indeed the more we know about play the more important that uncertainty seems to be (Lester and Russell, 2009). The concepts of risk, challenge and uncertainty intertwine in the landscape of play: none are fixed entities and they cross boundaries of emotional responses, social interactions and physical endeavour. They can be found in all types of play, not simply in physically-oriented play behaviours.

For example, scrambling up a play structure is a different challenge for a child with a visual impairment than for a child with an autistic spectrum disorder. Some children who use wheelchairs find the experience of sitting elsewhere (on grass, in sand, etc.) or being lifted and positioned personally risky. The experience of developing friendship and finding a place in play groupings can provoke a great deal of anxiety.

All of these contain elements of risk. In relation to physical risk (but perhaps equally relevant in all of the other areas) it has been said that 'Children with disabilities have an equal if not greater need for opportunities to take risks, since they may be denied the freedom of choice enjoyed by their non-disabled peers' (Play Safety Forum, 2002: 2).

There are of course reasons other than lack of freedom of choice: children with disabilities may have their access to play – and to becoming truly immersed in self-directed play – limited through lack of adequate environments, inadequate or the wrong type of support, over-protection, negative attitudes or low expectations of their abilities and aspirations.

Finding ways to support the qualities of risk, uncertainty and challenge in the outdoors is therefore based on understanding and responding to what these constitute for an individual child.

Image 9.3   Opportunities in the sandscape

 Case study – Sandpit to sandscape

Place: a play setting with a ¾ acre outdoor space, based on inclusive philosophy and practice.

Observation: the team became aware that some groups of children were less likely than others to access sand and water play. With a large sandpit (approximately 14m x 10m) and ready access to water, the sand and water play was a highly popular feature, offering a wide range of play experiences. Children with complex disabilities, particularly those using wheelchairs and some children with visual impairments, however, seemed to be missing out.

Analysis of the problem: after observing and talking with children, parents and other adults a number of barriers were identified:

- Most of these children relied on an adult to assist them to access sand and water play

- The sandpit wasn't seen as a place 'for them'

- Boisterous water play sometimes dominated and wet sand was less attractive for some children especially to sit in

- There was some reluctance to allow wheelchairs to get sandy

- Wheelchair access to the sand was difficult and not all children wanted to be transferred from their chair to the sand or cushions in it.

Process of engagement: a range of methods were used, including a large information and comment wall, planned conversations with children and adults, and focused observation of sand and water play recorded by all staff over a set period of time. Test surfaces were set up for the children to try out for accessibility, including wooden planks at various distances apart on the sand. Prototype sand tables were set up made from tyres and planks and tested by the children to find out what made them easy or difficult to reach. Digital recordings were made and reviewed revealing interesting aspects of adult support to children, physical movement and helpful and less helpful strategies already deployed.

Designing solutions: a newly designed 'sandscape' focuses on the way children are able to move through and around the whole space by creating a landscape of sand, grassy mounds, paths and some hard surfaces with adjustable platforms. It is larger and with 'blurry' edges making it more integrated with the overall play space. Changes in level mean that children seeking more contemplative play can do so without being overwhelmed by more dominating forms of play. Water is accessed by a pump requiring cooperation and a little effort to maintain a supply.

Observable results: the area is popular with all children and not identified as being for any particular group; new play has been sparked; interchangeable elements and adjustable heights mean steps can be taken to adjust the 'sandscape' as necessary for different children; there are limitless possibilities for creating and changing 'centres of interest'; adults are less reluctant to make use of sand and water opportunities; use of loose part elements adds an additional layer of complexity to the environmental possibilities.

Moving forward

 Things to think about and do

Risk and uncertainty: observation activity

Make up a simple observation sheet with the words 'challenge' 'risk' and 'uncertainty'. Carry out a few observations looking out for examples of:

- children taking themselves into a situation or experience of which the outcome is uncertain

- various types of risk and challenge

- children challenging their own limits – going faster, higher, being afraid but trying anyway

- adults' reactions to uncertainty, risk and challenge.

Spend some time with colleagues reflecting on these observations and consider whether the environment is providing adequate opportunities for all children, whether there are barriers, and what changes might be valuable.

(Continued)

(Continued)

Centres of interest: team task

In turn over the course of a number of weeks, allocate members of the team to set up 'centres of interest'. Use loose materials and ideas gleaned from observation of children's play or apply ideas from art or nature. Set up the 'centre of interest', then step back to watch and document. Create a 'centres of interest' compendium and use this as a basis for further reflection and planning.

Engage with the children

Engage with the children in figuring out how the environment should be adjusted or improved to remove barriers and enhance play. Spend a bit of time as a low-key presence in the play environment, playing when invited by the children. Avoid formulaic consultation which will result in formulaic responses.

The UN Convention on the Rights of the Child

Do some active reading to identify the links between the right to play, other aspects of the Convention and the goals of your setting. Consider the implications for policy and practice and write yourself some action points as a result.

Key messages

- Developing the play environment with the aim of supporting inclusion is a useful and very child-centred (and play-centred) strategy.

  o There may be factors in the play environment that make it difficult for a child to be part of play or conversely missing elements that could help them.

  o The range of play that the environment supports may be too narrow and therefore excludes the play preferences of some children.

- Instead of highlighting difference between children in a negative way, a good outdoor play environment can absorb and support diverse play behaviours. Inclusive environments are those in which it is possible to play in the varied ways that are satisfying the child at the time and that can accommodate children's different ways of being and expressing themselves.

- In properly paying attention to how inclusive the environment is, a richer play environment is created for all of the children who use it. Although there are very occasional dilemmas created by a tension between access, freedom and safe boundaries, on the whole the most inclusive environments are the most playful and rewarding for any child who comes to play.

Further reading and resources

Ball, D. Gill, T. and Spiegal, B. (2008) *Managing Risk in Play Provision: Implementation Guide.* London: Department for Children, Schools and Families.

Casey, T. (2010) *Inclusive Play – Practical Strategies for Children from Birth to Eight* (2nd edn). London: Sage.

The International Play Association: Promoting the Child's Right to Play: www.ipaworld.org

UNICEF (1989) Convention on the Rights of the Child: www.unicef.org/crc

10

Taking an active part

Everyday participation and effective consultation

Miranda Murray

This chapter explores:

- **The philosophy that states that young children's ideas and opinions should inform and influence decisions made regarding their outdoor play**
- **How practitioners can take an active role in encouraging participation and describes practical steps that can be taken to achieve this**
- **The numerous ways in which this value can be integrated into everyday practice. This chapter aims to provoke thought and debate around ways to effectively initiate such an approach**

Value: Young children should participate in decisions and actions affecting their outdoor play.

Young children should take an active part in decisions and actions for outdoor provision, big and small. Their perspectives and views are critical and must be sought, and they can take an active role in setting up, clearing away and caring for the outdoor space.

This value sets out explicitly the need for young children's active involvement in all aspects of outdoor practice and provision. This ranges from what they want to explore and play with, to the management, organisation and daily running of the outdoor provision. Children can and should be enabled to make decisions and take an active role in:

- the organisation, set up, running, tidying away and storage of resources. This would include decisions around what resources to use, where, when and how they can be used.

- the daily routines for play and learning, and care of the outdoor environment space, its equipment and resources.

- any longer term or bigger changes that may need to take place with the outdoor provision, such as the addition or removal of resources and any changes to the space itself.

The rationale for participation outdoors

Ensuring that children are given opportunities to take an active role and make decisions about their outdoor provision is fundamental to providing high quality early years practice and provision. But how do children benefit from becoming 'Managers of their own learning' (DCSF, 2007: 2)?

Everyday participation supports children in learning skills, attitudes and dispositions vital for their development into independent, autonomous individuals. Young children value being given opportunities to take the initiative and be involved in the care and upkeep of the outdoor area (Daycare Trust, 1998, quoted in Lindon, 2001: 66–7; Pascal and Bertram, 1997). By enabling them to make decisions that will affect their everyday lives, we actively show that we are listening to them, and that what they are saying to us matters and is being acted upon. This in turn helps to promote children's self-esteem and confidence. They are enabled to facilitate their own learning journeys and creative thinking skills as they plan, problem-solve, negotiate and make informed judgements in their self-led play. They are also supported to learn from the consequences of their actions, giving them vital opportunities for the development of resilience, which is an important life skill.

Habitual consultation and participation ensures that our practice and provision is relevant and caters directly to children's differing needs and interests, 'because it ensures that learning is matched to what they want to do and achieve' (DCSF, 2007: 2). Children are the best people to give you informed answers about themselves and their thoughts, feelings and interests. They are '... the experts in their own lives' (Langsted, 1994, quoted in Clark and Moss, 2001: 6). The answer to what will inspire, motivate and engage them needs to come directly from them rather than from an adult, as the two perspectives may vary considerably (Bishop et al., 1972, quoted in Titman, 1994: 111). Alison Clark developed a range of techniques called The Mosaic Approach (Clark and Moss, 2001) to find out young children's perspectives on aspects of their everyday lives. In one setting she found that the many of the children valued a particular outdoor space that the practitioners had previously considered an unimportant 'empty space'. If we do not involve children in making decisions about how they want to use their space, it is all too easy to overlook the importance of such areas to them.

Involving children in active decision-making transforms the adult role from supervisor, cleaner and director to enabler, facilitator and even co-player. By taking a 'hands off' approach, practitioners can focus instead on supporting children in making decisions for themselves. Adults gain time to properly 'scaffold' and extend learning through providing materials, resources and suggestions at the right point in the learning journey. This is a more effective and enjoyable role for adults and also helps to build children's skills, confidence and maturity through experiencing the process of decision making (Callaway, 2005).

> We have realised that it is important to find out from the children what they enjoy doing – in this way you can meet their needs directly. Very often we may have ideas

that we as adults think are wonderful, but the children don't actually enjoy them, and so that activity becomes redundant. By finding out what the children's interests and choices are you can avoid this. (Findon Valley Pre-school, Worthing) (Murray, 2007: 7)

Principles into practice

It is convenient here to consider three broad areas for involving children in taking an active part outdoors, although in reality there are many more ways in which to develop such rich potential for children's involvement in their own well-being and learning.

1. Organisation and management of outdoor space

Consider how resources can be stored, organised and accessed to best enable children to make their own decisions about what to use and when.

- Ensure that storage and organisation of resources is easy and accessible to all, clearly labelled in a visual way that all children can understand.

- What storage works well for the children in your setting? If a garden shed is used as the main storage solution, make sure they are happy to access it. Is it uncluttered and light, or does it need reorganising with any old, broken or unused resources removed?

- Make sure that storage units, doors and shelves or hooks are at the correct height for children to access independently by letting the children work out with you what height would work best.

- Involving children in organising and labelling offers authentic learning opportunities and will improve their use and care of the outdoor play resources.

Think about how to support children in making decisions about when they can go outside and for how long 'whatever the weather'.

- Organise the transition area (the area through which the children access the outdoor space) so that they can easily and independently go out and in.

- Support children in deciding what clothing is needed to go outside 'today'. For example, have coat pegs by the door, named and at the child's level. Remember that role-modelling is an important learning tool – do practitioners have appropriate wet weather clothing?

- Provide a variety of different types of wet weather gear that will support different children's likes, dislikes, needs or abilities.

Let children decide how the space is used.

- Allow children to decide how they want the outdoor environment to be organised and used.

- Observe and respond to what children are 'telling you'. Are there secret, special places that the children have created such as under bushes and trees, behind sheds or any 'wild' spaces? Give them the opportunities to make such places and claim them as their own through being flexible with the use of the area and remembering not to overdevelop the area.

Image 10.1   Children contributing to ongoing management – making compost

 Case study – A playgroup in the south of England

The children at this setting spent a large amount of their day asking when it was time to go outside. Staff recognised that they needed to re-examine the daily routine of outside play for one whole-group session of just 30 minutes. They decided that they needed to act on the children's current interests in wanting to be outdoors for longer periods of time. A rolling snack time, where children could choose to go and have snack when they wanted to, was introduced and a member of staff was deployed in the outdoor area throughout the session. Movable dressing rails were also placed near the door to the outside for children to get their coats from themselves. These changes to the running and organisation of the setting enabled the children to have freely chosen and longer periods of time outdoors and consequently feel listened too and involved in the day-to-day decisions about their lives.

2. Involvement in short-term and daily decision-making

Support their role in deciding what the space is going to look like today and what 'journey' the learning is going to take.

- Give children choices about how they would like to set up the space or areas in it on a daily basis rather than setting it up for them beforehand.

- Be aware that some children can feel overwhelmed and intimidated by big decisions. For these children aim to give them small stages or smaller options which can be expanded as and when their confidence grows, for example, by focusing on one small area for them to set up.

- Even very young children and babies can play an active role in decisions about what they would like to do outdoors. For more ideas specifically for this age

Image 10.2   Children having responsibility for daily care tasks

group read *Listening as a Way of Life: Listening to Babies* by Diane Rich (see further reading below).

Enable children to take an active role in the daily care of plants, equipment, resources and the space itself.

- Ensure that proper children's tools are provided and help children learn how to use these effectively and safely.

- Keep the tools in places that children can get to easily as and when they feel that they are needed.

- Watering, weeding, sweeping up spilt sand or washing dirty equipment ensures that children take an active role not only in the care of the environment and its resources but also in their own care and safety. Children often take great satisfaction from routines and tasks that they perceive as adults jobs.

   Case study – A preschool in the south of England

Staff found that they were constantly asking the children to not play in an unused doorway in this outdoor space. Some felt that it was dangerous and were concerned that the children were not clearly visible. They decided that they needed to find out why the children wanted to play in it. Observation of play in the rest of the outdoor area highlighted that there were no other 'secret spaces' for children to use. It was clear that the children gravitated towards the doorway because it lent itself as a space that they could hide and feel enclosed in. Staff recognised that this experience was important to the children and they acknowledged that they needed to address how they could provide such experiences for the children in a way in which everyone would feel comfortable.

3. Involvement in long-term or strategic development of the outdoor provision

Ensure that children take an active role in developing any ideas for change.

- Use a range of different strategies to gather ideas from the children about how they feel and use the space now, for example asking the children to take photographs of their favourite and not so favourite spaces, or taking a teddy bear on a tour of the space. For more ideas on consultation techniques with young children read *Creating a Space to Grow: Developing your Outdoor Learning Environment* by Gail Ryder-Richardson and *Spaces to Play: More Listening to Young Children Using the Mosaic Approach* by Alison Clark and Peter Moss (see further reading below).

- Use this accumulated information to agree on what you need to keep the same and what could be changed. Ensure that you problem-solve any particular issues that need to be addressed together.

Involve children in making the changes and reviewing them.

- Children can play a role in implementing many of the changes decided, and again this holds rich potential for learning. Painting, digging, measuring out and marking etc. are all ways that children can be successfully and safely involved, making any changes more meaningful for the children and more valuable for learning and development.

- Ensure that any changes are evaluated by and with the children, as they are the users of the space and able to tell you what has worked and what needs to be adapted.

Case study – Reception year, a primary school in the south of England

In order to gather ideas for how to improve an uninspiring outdoor playground, practitioners at this setting decided to hold a 'stay and play' session. Resource boxes filled with low cost, open-ended resources were placed in the outdoor area for parents, governors, staff and children to explore. At the end of the session everyone was asked to show what they enjoyed the most by a 'run around' that finished at their chosen box. Children also tried out practical problem-solving for, 'where can we go when we want to ride our bikes?' and, 'where can we keep all our toys and materials so that we can get them easily when we need to?'

A teddy bear called 'Outdoors Oscar' was taken on a tour of the outdoors by the children (a tool in Learning through Landscapes, 2009). His tour was recorded in a scrapbook using photographs taken by the children with disposable cameras. This was used to promote discussion in class, and feed into the final design ideas for the area.

Image 10.3   Outdoor Oscar being taken on a tour

Moving forward

 Things to think about and do

Remember that enabling children to play an active role is something that needs to happen all day, everyday. It should be embedded in your everyday practice – from hanging up the coats to choices about play and changes to areas. Children's involvement should always be fun and meaningful rather than a task to be done to ensure that this box is ticked. Be creative in how you support children's participation and involvement recognising that children communicate in different ways. Lastly, always give feedback on what the children suggest and do not dismiss their ideas and thoughts lightly. Below are some ideas that you may want to try to get started.

- As a staff body take time to share memories of play outdoors as a child. What did you like to do; who and what did you chose to play with; how long did you choose to play outdoors, and did the weather affect your decisions? Was there much adult involvement? How did this impact on you as an adult? Compare your experiences of choice in your play to those that children have nowadays. How different are they? How can your setting give children the experience of choice and decision-making?

- Reflect on what you all feel the role of the practitioner is in your outdoor environment. Is it an enabler, facilitator, or co-player? What benefits does this have to the children in your setting? Can you come to an agreed definition and what does this look like in practice?

(Continued)

(Continued)

- Review your daily routines. Do they follow the needs and interests of the children or the staff? Do they need adapting to support the interests and needs of the current children in the group (see the case study Getting outdoors, p. 108)?

- Find out from the children their thoughts and opinions on the current outdoor space and how it is used. Give the children disposable or digital cameras and ask them to take photographs of places that are important to them outdoors. Discuss with them what they have taken photographs of and why. What do they feel about these places? Do they like them because of the play opportunities or because their friends enjoy playing there? Does the area look different from a child's level, for example, metal fencing obscuring views? Are there any unexpected outcomes, such as children valuing areas that you had not noticed?

- Review your current resources and storage. Involve the children in making an audit of the current resources and how they are stored. Is anything broken or not used regularly? Does it take up too much space? Are resources easily accessible? If not then consider what would work more effectively. Can you think of any ways to store resources that help children in tidying away independently?

Key messages

Enabling children to play an active part in daily decisions that effect their outdoor environments is fundamental to good quality practice and provision. This supports children in becoming creative, independent and confident managers of their own learning, and moves the adult role forward from director to enabler.

To successfully achieve this, settings need to create opportunities to make the most of supporting children in becoming active decision makers:

- Ensure that your outdoor storage is clear, accessible and understood by all children.

- Think about how to organise both your practice and provision to give children freedom of choice over where to go in their learning environment, for the time periods that they need, as their play unfolds.

- Support children in making decisions about their own play and learning by giving them freedom of choice over what to play with or explore. Think about how the practitioner's role best supports children in following their own interests.

- Be flexible with planning; base it around children's current interests and needs, adapting as and when special opportunities arise.

- Foster an overall attitude of inclusion, openness and communication between children, staff and parents.

- Ensure that you support all children to be involved and consulted in decision-making and participation through the use of different strategies and methods.

- Share your setting's policy of supporting children in active decision-making with the child's future setting or class at transition times, so that these skills and attitudes can be built on and developed further.

Further reading and resources

Ryder-Richardson, G. (2005) *Creating a Space to Grow: The Process of Developing Your Outdoor Learning Environment*. London: David Fulton.

Casey, T. (2007) *Environments for Outdoor Play*. London: Paul Chapman Publishers.

Rich, D. (2004) *Listening as a Way of Life: Listening to Babies*. London: National Children's Bureau.

Clark, A. and Moss, P. (2005) *Spaces to Play: More Listening to Young Children Using the Mosaic Approach*. London: National Children's Bureau.

Learning through Landscapes (2009) *Play Out: A Guide to Developing Your Early Years Outdoors*. Devon: Southgate Publishers Ltd. Available at: www.ltl.org.uk

Learning through Landscapes, *Early Years Outdoors*: www.ltl.org.uk

References

Abbott, L. and Nutbrown, C. (eds) (2001) *Experiencing Reggio Emilia: Implications for Pre-school Provision*. Buckingham: Open University Press.

Adolph, K., Vereijken, B. and Shrout, P. (2003) 'What changes in infant walking and why', *Child Development*, 74(2): 475–97.

Arnold, C. and the Pen Green Team (2010) *Understanding Schemas and Emotion in Early Childhood*. London: Sage.

Athey, C. (1990) *Extending Thought in Young Children*. London: Paul Chapman.

Ball, D., Gill, T. and Spiegal, B. (2008) *Managing Risk in Play Provision: Implementation Guide*. London: Department for Children, Schools and Families.

Bilton, H. (2002) *Outdoor Play in the Early Years: Management and Innovation* (2nd edn). London: David Fulton.

Bilton, H. (2010) *Outdoor Learning in the Early Years: Management and Innovation* (3rd edn). London: David Fulton Publishers.

Brady, L., Gibb, J., Henshall, A. and Lewis, J. (2008) *Play and Exercise in Early Years: Physically Active Play in Early Childhood Provision*. NCB/Play England, Department of Culture, Media and Sport. Available at: http://www.culture.gov.uk/reference_library/research-and-statistics/5215.aspx

Broadhead, P. (2003) *Early Years Play and Learning: Developing Social Skills and Cooperation*. Abingdon, Oxon: Routledge.

Brown, F. (2003) *Playwork: Theory and Practice*. Maidenhead, Berkshire: Open University Press.

Brown, F. and Taylor, C. (eds) (2008) *Foundations of Playwork*. Maidenhead, Berkshire: Open University Press.

Brown, S. (2009) *Play: How it Shapes the Brain, Opens the Imagination and Invigorates the Soul*. London: Penguin Group.

Bruce, T. (1987) *Early Childhood Education*. London: Hodder & Stoughton.

Bruce, T. (1991) *Time to Play in Early Childhood Education*. London: Hodder & Stoughton.

Bruce, T. (2001) *Learning through Play: Babies, Toddlers and the Foundation Years*. London: Hodder & Stoughton.

Bruce, T. (2009) *Early Childhood Practice*, Volume 10(2).

Bundy, A., Luckett, T., Tranter, P., Naughton, A., Wyver, S., Razen, J. and Spies, G. (2009) 'The risk is that there is no risk: A simple, innovative intervention to increase children's activity levels', *International Journal of Early Years Education*, 17(1): 33–45.

Caillois, R. (2001) *Man, Play and Games* (trans. M. Barash). Urbana, IL: University of Illinois Press.

Callaway, G. (2005) *The Early Years Curriculum: A View from the Outdoors*. London: David Fulton.

Carr, M. (2001) *Assessment in Early Childhood Settings*. London: Paul Chapman.

Carson, R. (1998) *The Sense of Wonder*. New York: HarperCollins Publishers.

Casey, T. (2007) *Environments for Outdoor Play – A Practical Guide to Making Space for Children*. London: Sage.

CCEA (Council for the Curriculum, Examinations and Assessment) (2007) *The Northern Ireland Curriculum: Primary*. Belfast: CCEA Publications. Available at: www.nicurriculum.org.uk/foundation_stage (accessed May 2010).

Chilvers, D. (2006) *Young Children Talking: The Art of Conversation and Why Children Need to Chatter*. London: The British Association for Early Childhood Education.

Clark, A. and Moss, P. (2001) *Listening to Young Children: The Mosaic Approach*. London: National Children's Bureau.

Claxton, G. (1998) *Hare Brain, Tortoise Mind: Why Intelligence Increases When You Think Less*. London: Fourth Estate.

Claxton, G. (1999) *Wise Up: The Challenge of Life-long Learning*. London: Bloomsbury.

Cobb, E. (1977) *The Ecology of Imagination in Childhood*. New York: Columbia University Press.

Corsaro, W.A. (2005) *The Sociology of Childhood* (2nd edn). London: Sage.

Cousins, J. (1999) *Listening to Four Year Olds*. London: National Early Years Network (NCB).

Craft, A. (2002) *Creativity and Early Years Education: A Life Wide Foundation*. London: Continuum.

Csikszentmihalyi, M. (1975) *Beyond Boredom and Anxiety: Experiencing Flow in Work and Play*. San Francisco: Jossey-Bass.

Cullen, J. (1993) 'Preschool children's use and perceptions of outdoor play areas', *Early Childhood Education and Care*, 89(1): 45–56.

Curtis, D. and Carter, M. (2003) *Designs for Living and Learning: Transforming Early Childhood Environments*. St Paul, MN: Redleaf Press.

Daycare Trust (1998) *Listening to Children – Young Children's Views on Childcare: A Guide for Parents*. London: Daycare Trust.

DCSF (2007) Early Years Foundation Stage: *Active Learning – In Depth*. Available at: http://nationalstrategies.standards.dcsf.gov.uk/node/84341?uc=force_uj

DCSF (2008a) *Every Child Matters Outcomes Framework*. London: DCSF.

DCSF (2008b) *Statutory Framework for the Early Years Foundation Stage*. London: DCSF.

DCSF (2008c) *The Early Years Foundation Stage Effective Practice: Outdoor Learning*. London: HMSO.

DfES (2006) *Learning Outside the Classroom Manifesto*. London: DfES. Available at: www.lotc.org.uk (accessed May 2010).

Doddington, C. and Hilton, M. (2007) *Child-Centred Education: Reviving the Creative Tradition*. London: Sage.

Doherty, J. and Whiting, M. (2004) 'All about tackling childhood obesity', *Nursery World*, 1 April.

Dweck, C. (2000) *Self Theories: Their Role in Motivation, Personality and Development*. Hove: Psychology Press.

Edgington, M. (2002) *The Great Outdoors*. London: Early Education.

Edwards, C., Gandini, L. and Forman, G. (1998) *The Hundred Languages of Children*. Westport, CT: Ablex Publishing Corporation.

Every Disabled Child Matters, *Inclusion Charter*. Available at: www.edcm.org.uk

Featherstone, S. (ed.), Louis, S., Beswick, C., Magraw, L. and Hayes, L. (2008) *Again! Again! Understanding Schemas in Young Children*. London: A & C Black Publishing.

Flemmen, A. (2001) 'Real play', *Play Rights* XXII.

Gardner, H. (1999) *Intelligence Reframed: Multiple Intelligences for the 21st Century*. New York: Basic Books.

Garrick, R. (2009) *Playing Outdoors in the Early Years* (2nd edn). London, New York: Continuum.

Gibson, J. (1979) *The Ecological Approach to Visual Perception*. Hillsdale, NJ: Laurence Erlbaum.

Goddard Blythe, S. (2008) *What Children Really Need*. Stroud: Hawthorne Press.

Greenland, P. (2006) 'Physical development', in T. Bruce (ed.) *Early Childhood: A Guide for Students*. London: Sage.

Holloway, S. and Valentine, G. (eds) (2000) *Children's Geographies: Playing, Living, Learning*. London and New York: Routledge.

Holme, A. and Massie, P. (1970) *Children's Play: A Study of Needs and Opportunities*. London: Michael Joseph Ltd.

Isaacs, S. (1930) *Intellectual Growth in Young Children*. London: Routledge & Kegan Paul Ltd.

Kalliala, M. (2006) *Play Culture in a Changing World*. Maidenhead: Open University Press.

Kindlon, D. and Thompson, M. (2000) *Raising Cain: Protecting the Emotional Life of Boys*. New York, Toronto: Ballantine Publishing Group.

Kloep, M. and Hendry, L. (2007) '"Over-protection, over-protection, over-protection!" Young people in modern Britain', *Psychology of Education Review*, 31(2): 4–8.

Knight, S. (2009) *Forest Schools and Outdoor Learning in the Early Years*. London: Sage.

Laevers, F., Vandenbussche, E., Kog, M. and Depondt, L. (2006) *A Process-oriented Child Monitoring System for Young Children*. Leuven, Belgium: CEGO.

Langsted, O. (1994) 'Looking at quality from the child's perspective', in P. Moss and A. Pence (eds) *Valuing Quality in Early Childhood Services: New Approaches to Defining Quality*. London: Paul Chapman.

Lasenby, M. (1990) *The Early Years: A Curriculum for Young Children – Outdoor Play*. London: Marcourt Brace Jovanovich.

Lawrence, E. (ed.) (1969) *Freidrich Froebel and English Education*. London: Routledge and Kegan Paul.

Learning through Landscapes (2009) *Play Out: A Guide to Developing Your Early Years Outdoors*. Devon: Southgate Publishers Ltd. Available at: http://www.ltl.org.uk

Lester, S. and Maudsley, M. (2006) *Play, Naturally: A Review of Children's Natural Play*. London: Children's Play Council.

Lester, S. and Russell, W. (2009) *Play for a Change*. London: Play England.

Lindon, J. (2001) *Understanding Children's Play*. Cheltenham: Nelson Thornes.

Lindon, J. (2003) *Too Safe for their Own Good? Helping Children Learn about Risks and Lifeskills*. London: National Children's Bureau.

Little, H. (2006) 'Children's risk taking behaviour: Implications for early childhood policy and practice', *International Journal of Early Years Education*, 14(2): 141–54.

McIntyre, S. (2007) *People Play Together More: A Handbook for Supporting Inclusive Play*. Edinburgh: The Yard.

McMillan, M. (1919) *The Nursery School*. London: J.M. Dent & Sons Ltd.

Madge, N. and Barker, J. (2007) *Risk and Childhood*. London: RSA.

Maxwell, L., Mitchell, M. and Evans, G. (2008) 'Effects of play equipment and loose parts on preschool children's outdoor play behavior: An observational study and design intervention', *Children, Youth and Environments*, 18(2): 33–63.

Medina, J. (2008) *Brain Rules: 12 Principles for Surviving and Thriving at Work, Home and School*. Seattle, WA: Pear Press.

Mental Health Foundation (1999) *Bright Futures: Promoting Children and Young People's Mental Health*. London: Mental Health Foundation.

Ministry of Education (1996) *Te Whāriki*. Wellington: Learning Media.

Moss, P. and Petrie, P. (2002) *From Children's Services to Children's Spaces*. London: Routledge.

Muñoz, S.A. (2009) *Children Outdoors: A Literature Review*. Forres, Scotland: Sustainable Development Research Centre.

Murray, M. (2007) *West Sussex Outdoors For All. A Celebration*. Winchester: Learning through Landscapes.

Murray, R. and O'Brien, L. (2005) *'Such Enthusiasm – a joy to see': An Evaluation of Forest School in England.* Report to the Forestry Commission. Available at: http://www.forestresearch.gov.uk/pdf/ForestSchoolEnglandReport.pdf/$FILE/ForestSchoolEnglandReport.pdf

National Children's Bureau (2006) *Inclusive Play Factsheet.* London: NCB.

NCCA (National Council for Curriculum Assessment) (2010) *Siolta – the National Quality Framework for Early Childhood Education, and Aistear – the Early Childhood Curriculum Framework.* Available at: www.ncca.ie/earlychildhoodframework (accessed May 2010).

Nutbrown, C. (1996) *Children's Rights and Early Education.* London: Paul Chapman Publishing.

Office of the Deputy Prime Minister (2004) *Developing Accessible Play Space: A Good Practice Guide.* London: Office of the Deputy Prime Minister.

Ofsted (2006) *Early Years: Safe and Sound.* HMI 2663. Available at: www.ofsted.gov.uk (accessed 3 April 2007).

Ouvry, M. (2003) *Exercising Muscles and Minds: Outdoor Play in the Early Years Curriculum.* London: National Children's Bureau.

Palmer, J.A. and Birch, J.C. (2004) *Geography in the Early Years* (2nd edn). London: Routledge.

Parsons, G. (2007) *Heading Out: Exploring the Impact of Outdoor experiences on Young Children.* Winchester: Learning through Landscapes.

Pascal, C. and Bertram, T. (eds) (1997) *Effective Early Learning: Case Studies in Improvement.* London: Hodder & Stoughton.

Pearce, J.C. (1977) *Magical Child: Rediscovering Nature's Plan for our Children.* New York: E.P. Dutton.

Perry, J.P. (2001) *Outdoor Play: Teaching Strategies with Young Children.* New York: Teachers College Press.

Play Safety Forum (2002) *Managing Risk in Play Provision: A Position Statement.* London: Children's Play Council.

QCA (2000) *Curriculum Guidance for the Foundation Stage.* London: QCA.

Rich, D., Casanova, D., Dixon, A., Drummond, M.J., Durrant, A. and Myer, C. (2005) *First Hand Experience: What Matters to Children.* Suffolk: Rich Learning Opportunities.

Rich, D., Drummond, M.J. and Myer, C. (2008) *Learning: What Matters to Children.* Suffolk: Rich Learning Opportunities.

Roberts, R. (2010) *Wellbeing from Birth.* London: Sage.

Robinson, K. and Aronica, L. (2009) *The Element: How Finding Your Passion Changes Everything.* London: Penguin Books.

Sandseter, E. (2007) 'Categorising risky play: How can we identify risk taking in children's play?' *European Early Childhood Research,* 15(2): 237–52.

Sandseter, E. (2009) 'Children's expressions of exhilaration and fear in risky play', *Contemporary Issues in Early Childhood* 10(2). Available at: www.wwwords.co.uk/CIEC (accessed 16 June 2009).

Scottish Executive (2007) *A Curriculum for Excellence: Building the Curriculum 2: Active Learning in the Early Years.* Available at: www.ltscotland.org.uk/curriculumforexcellence/curriculumoverview/index.asp (accessed May 2010).

Sebba, R. (1991) 'The landscapes of childhood: The reflection of childhood's environment in adult memories and in children's attitudes', *Environment and Behavior,* 23(4): 395–422.

Sightlines (2008) *Doing the Right Thing,* DVD. Available at: www.sightlines-initiative.com

Siraj-Blatchford, I. and Sylva, K. (2004) 'Researching pedagogy in English Pre-schools', *British Educational Research Journal,* 30(5): 713–30.

Siraj-Blatchford, I., Sylva, K., Muttock, S., Gilden, R. and Bell, D. (2002) *Researching Effective Pedagogy in the Early Years*. Research Report 356. Oxford: Department of Educational Studies, University of Oxford.

Spinka, M., Newberry, R. and Bekoff, M. (2001) 'Mammalian play: Training for the unexpected', *The Quarterly Review of Biology*, 76(2): 141–68.

Stephenson, A. (2003) 'Physical risk taking: dangerous or endangered?', *Early Years*, 23(1): 35–43.

Stock Kranowitz, C. (2005) *The Out-of-Sync Child: Recognising and Coping with Sensory Processing Disorder*. New York: Perigee Books.

Storr, A. (1989) *Solitude*. London: Collins.

Sutherland, M. (2008) *Developing the Gifted and Talented Young Learner*. London: Sage.

Sustainable Development Commission (2007) *Every Child's Future Matters*. London: SDC.

Titman, W. (1994) *Special Places, Special People: The Hidden Curriculum of the School Grounds*. Hampshire: World Wildlife Fund/Learning through Landscapes.

Titman, W. (2009) Nursery World conference speech, London, November.

Tovey, H. (2007) *Playing Outdoors: Spaces and Places, Risk and Challenge*. Maidenhead: Open University Press.

Tovey, H. (2010) 'Playing on the edge: Perceptions of risk and danger in outdoor play', in P. Broadhead, J. Howard and E. Woods (eds) *Play and Learning in the Early Years: From Research to Practice*. London. Sage.

United Nations Committee on the Rights of the Child (2005) *General Comment No.7: Implementing Child Rights in Early Childhood*. Geneva: United Nations. Available at: http://www2.ohchr.org/english/bodies/crc/comments.htm

United Nations Committee on the Rights of the Child (2006) *General Comment No.9: The Rights of Disabled Children*. Geneva: United Nations. Available at: http://www2.ohchr.org/english/bodies/crc/comments.htm

Vision & Values Partnership (2004) *Early Years Vision and Values for Outdoor Play*. Available as a copyright-free download at: www.ltl.org.uk

WAG (Welsh Assembly Government) (2008) *Framework for Children's Learning for 3- to 7-year-olds in Wales*. Cardiff: Welsh Assembly Government.

Waite, S., Davis, B. and Brown, K. (2006) *Current Practice and Aspirations for Outdoor Learning for 2–11 Year Olds in Devon*. Consultation Report June 2006. University of Plymouth.

Waller, T. (2007) '"The trampoline tree and the swamp monster with 18 heads": Outdoor play in the Foundation Stage and Foundation Phase', *Education 3–13*, 35(4): 395–409.

Waller, T. (2009) 'Outdoor play and learning', in T. Waller (ed.) *An Introduction to Early Childhood: A Multi-disciplinary Approach* (2nd edn). London: Sage.

Ward, C. (1988) *The Child in the Country*. London: Bedford Square Press.

Warden, C. (2007) *Nurture through Nature*. Auchterader: Mindstretchers.

White, J. (2008) *Playing and Learning Outdoors: Making Provision for High Quality Experiences in the Outdoor Environment*. Abingdon, Oxon & New York: Routledge.

Wilson, F.R. (1998) *The Hand: How Its Use Shapes the Brain, Language and Human Culture*. New York: Vintage Books.

Wilson, R. (1997) 'The wonders of nature: Honouring children's ways of knowing', *Early Childhood News*, 6(19). Available at: http://www.earlychildhoodnews.com/earlychildhood/articles_view.aspx?ArticleId=7.

Index

RISK AND ADVENTURE IN EARLY YEARS OUTDOOR PLAY

Learning from Forest Schools

Sara Knight *Anglia Ruskin University*

Do you want to create exciting outdoor experiences for children? Are you looking for guidance on how to incorporate the wilder and riskier elements of outdoor play into your planning?

This book will give you the confidence to offer the children in your setting adventurous and challenging outdoor activities, as well as ways to utilize natural resources to their best advantage. There is clear, practical advice on what you need to do, which is underpinned by the theory that supports the benefits of this approach. Examples from settings are included, to illustrate best practice and to show how things can be achieved.

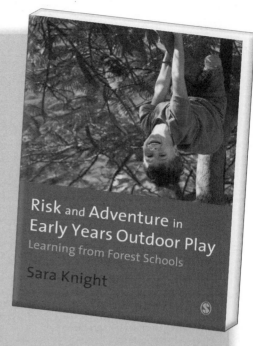

Issues considered include:

- being outside in bad weather
- the importance of risk-taking
- the benefits of rough-and-tumble play
- observing and assessing children in this mode
- how these experiences improve children's learning
- explaining activities to parents, colleagues and managers
- ensuring health and safety requirements are met
- the role of the adult in facilitating these experiences.

Suitable for all students and practitioners working with young children from birth to eight years , this book will not only give you ideas for outdoor play but also help you understand exactly what you are doing, why it is educationally sound and developmentally important for children, and where it connects with the Early Years Foundation Stage in England, the Foundation Phase in Wales and the Curriculum for Excellence in Scotland .

April 2011 • 152 pages
Cloth (978-1-84920-629-7) • £60.00
Paper (978-1-84920-630-3) • £19.99

ALSO FROM SAGE